LONDON DIARY

Peter Bialobrzeski

December 1 – December 8, 2022

Hartmann books

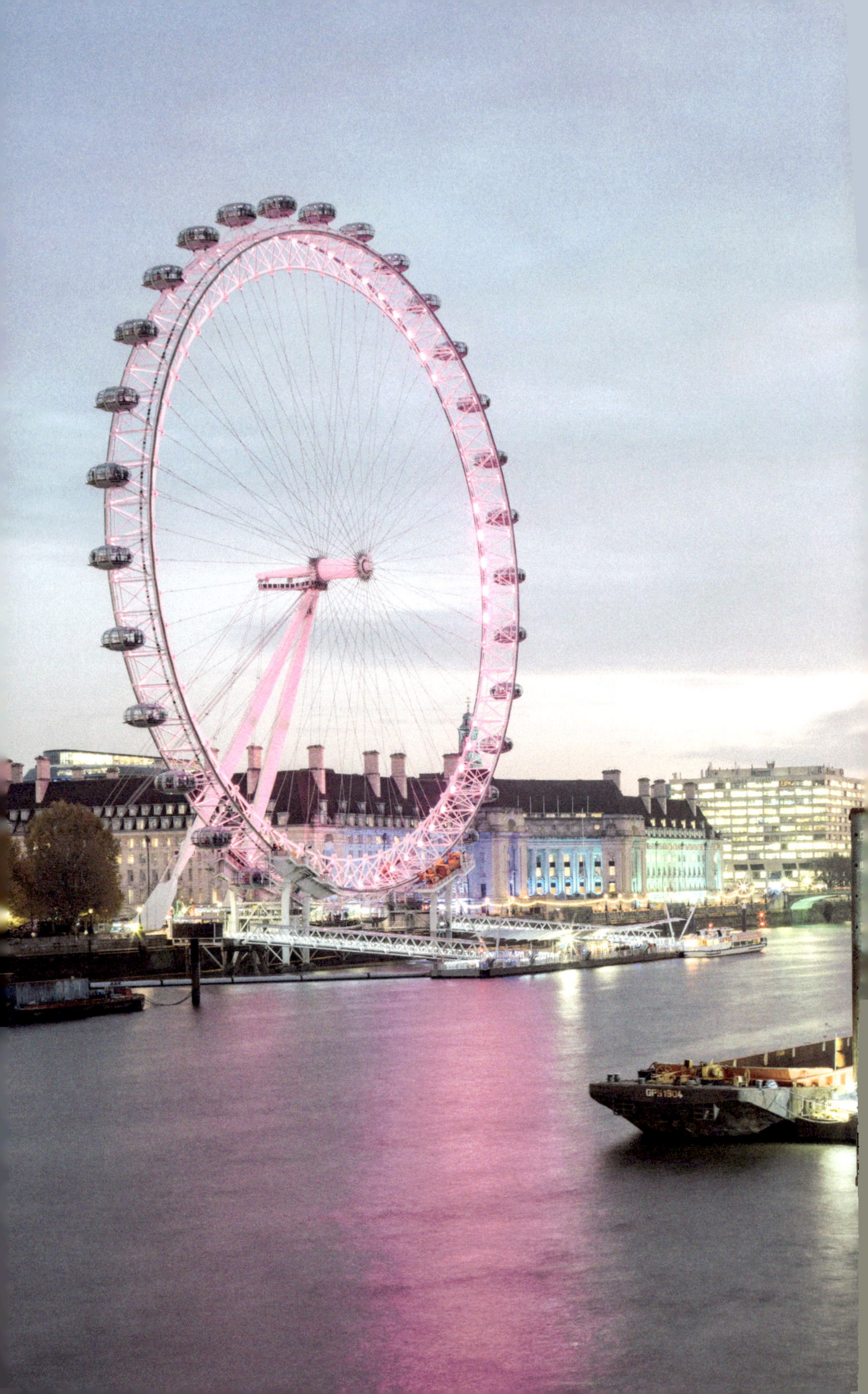
GPS1904

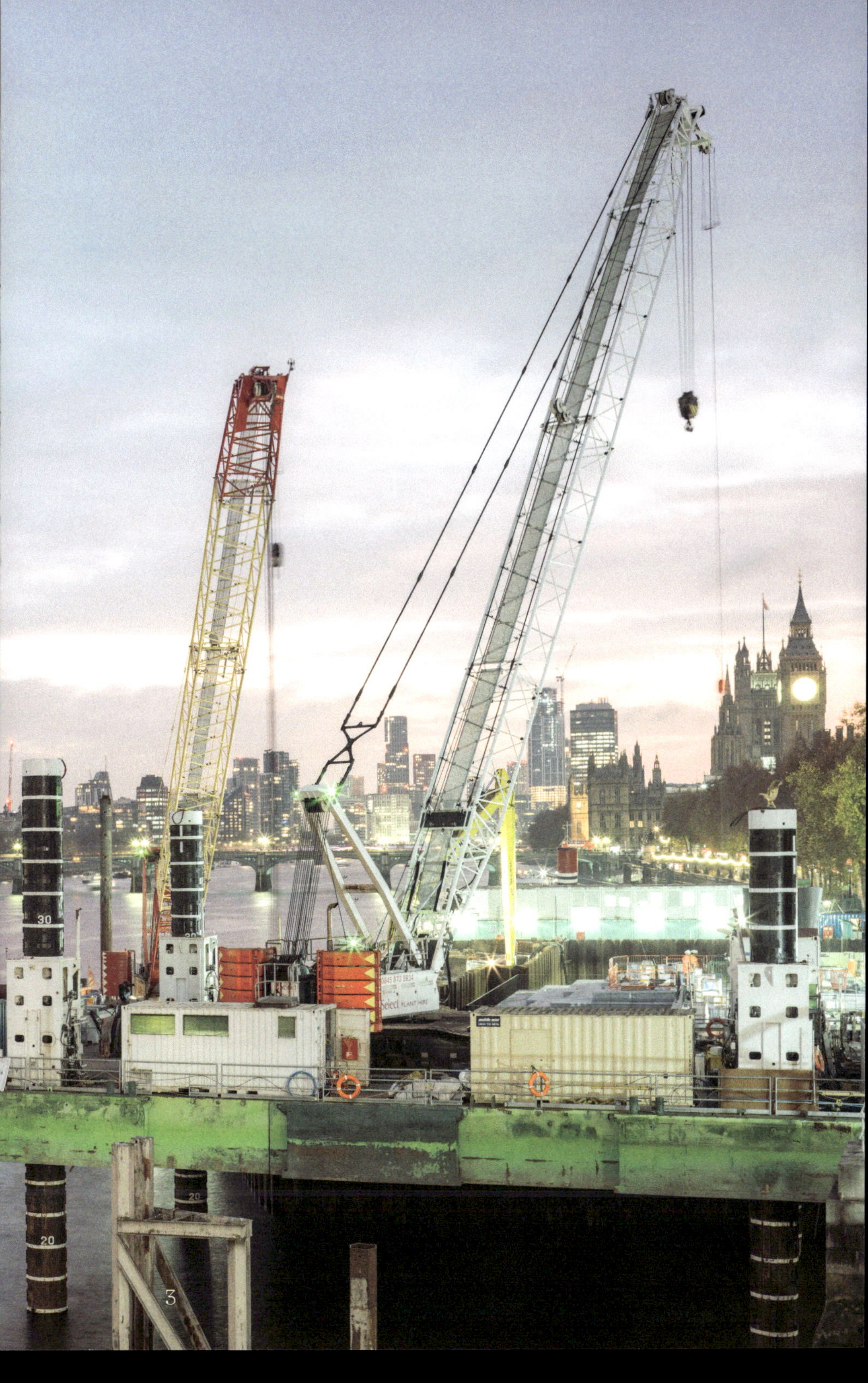
30
20
20
Select

LONDON DIARY
Peter Bialobrzeski

→December 1, 2022 It is has been nearly thirty years since I left the city after having lived here for almost a year. Today, the megalopolis presents itself very differently. *The City*, the financial and economic hub, is slowly but steadily turning into a kind of Singapore. And I keep thinking, oh yes, this is why they left the EU. They can hardly walk because of their strength. The tube stations spit out a workforce that makes just enough money to consume their takeaway lattes, followed by a *Pret-A-Manger* sandwich. In the morning, at least, *The City* feels like a self-sufficient machine, squeezing the last drop of blood out of the many to make money for the few.
→December 2, 2022 Despite the fact that capitalism is flexing its muscles all over town, there is an enormous amount of energy all over the place. Back home in Gemany, the media presents an image of London and Britain being in a state of despair and economic downturn. Sorry folks, it does not feel that way! But here comes the downside: According to *The Guardian*, an East London couple is facing eviction from their three-bedroom flat because they refused to pay a sixtypercent rent increase. The three thousand pounds a month that the landlord is asking for is more than the couple's combined income.
→December 3, 2022 On this freezing morning I find myself near Tottenham Court Road station at 7:30 a.m. The hungry and the homeless, the mentally disturbed, and the facility workers occupy the scene at this very hour. A far cry from Harry and Meghan's *bombshell trailer* for their forthcoming Netflix documentary, which is reviewed extensively in the *Evening Standard*. More gossip: Boris Johnson plans to stay in politics and has announced that he will run for a seat in his West London constituency. Rumor has it that he has been asked by *The Telegraph* to write a weekly opinion piece. →December 4, 2022 Following the Chinese government's successful acquisition of prime real estate in Tower Hamlets, the local council has voted against the proposed construction of a new Chinese embassy. Councillor Simon Cheng said after the vote: "I think the Hong Kong community and many others—Uighur Muslims, Tibetans, and even our Chinese community—will be happy about this." And the Chinese? Are not amused.→December 5, 2022 Walking through the borough of Hackney, I keep thinking that London is shamelessly

transforming itself into a city only for the rich. Apartment buildings called *The Makers* and *The Principal* are spreading their legs to welcome the chosen few who can afford to pay a million pounds for a two-bedroom flat. Meanwhile, the government is trying to close a legal loophole that allows foreign diplomats from the Global South to exploit their domestic workers. Even though it happens on British territory, the perpetrators claim immunity. Newspapers are calling it modern slavery. →December 6, 2022 The transformation of London is noticeable in the vast amount number of new pedestrian zones. These are newly paved by the surrounding estates. Countless times I am reminded by very polite security guards that it is okay to take pictures, but not to use a tripod. The municipalities do not have to pay for the construction, maintenance, and security of these areas. Instead, the jurisdiction lies with private real estate companies that use tons of CCTV cameras to monitor their property. According to the website *caughtoncamera.net,* the average Londoner is watched an estimated three hundred times a day! In total, there are around half a million CCTV cameras operating throughout the city.

→December 7, 2022 On my way to East London, I see an advertisement, on the Tube that reads *muslimmarriagesolution.com*. The mosque in Whitechapel must have been recently renovated; it matches the colors of the neighboring *Ibisbudget* hotel. The Muslim grocery and vegetable shops I remember have disappeared. The steel-and-glass towers of *The City* keep moving eastward. Meanwhile, a couple that has long left London but is still incredibly present has been awarded the *Ripple of Hope Award* alongside President Volodymyr Zelenskyy of Ukraine. Meghan and Harry presumably did not meet through *muslimmarriagesolution.com*.
→December 8, 2022 The saga continues. It is the day of the revelation. The media speculate that Charles III, the father of the Duke of Sussex, will sit in front of a royal screen to see what his daughter-in-law has to reveal that goes beyond the infamous Oprah Winfrey interview. Another seemingly male character has hit the streets and the news: *The Troll from Trondheim*, will make London's temperatures plummet to four degrees below zero, according to the *Evening Standard*. Nice name for a cold front, I guess, and I decide to stay warm.

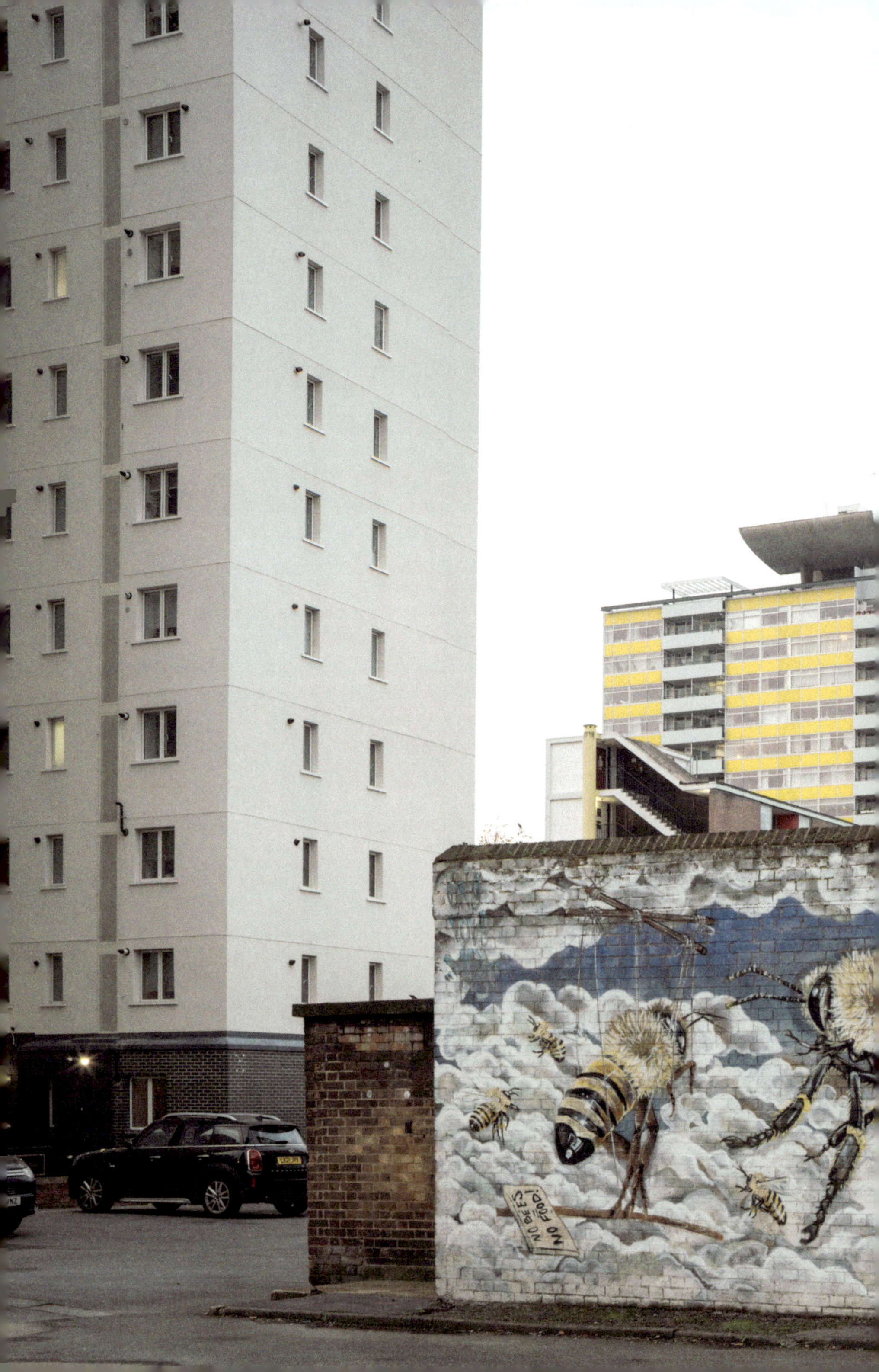
NO BEES
NO FOOD!

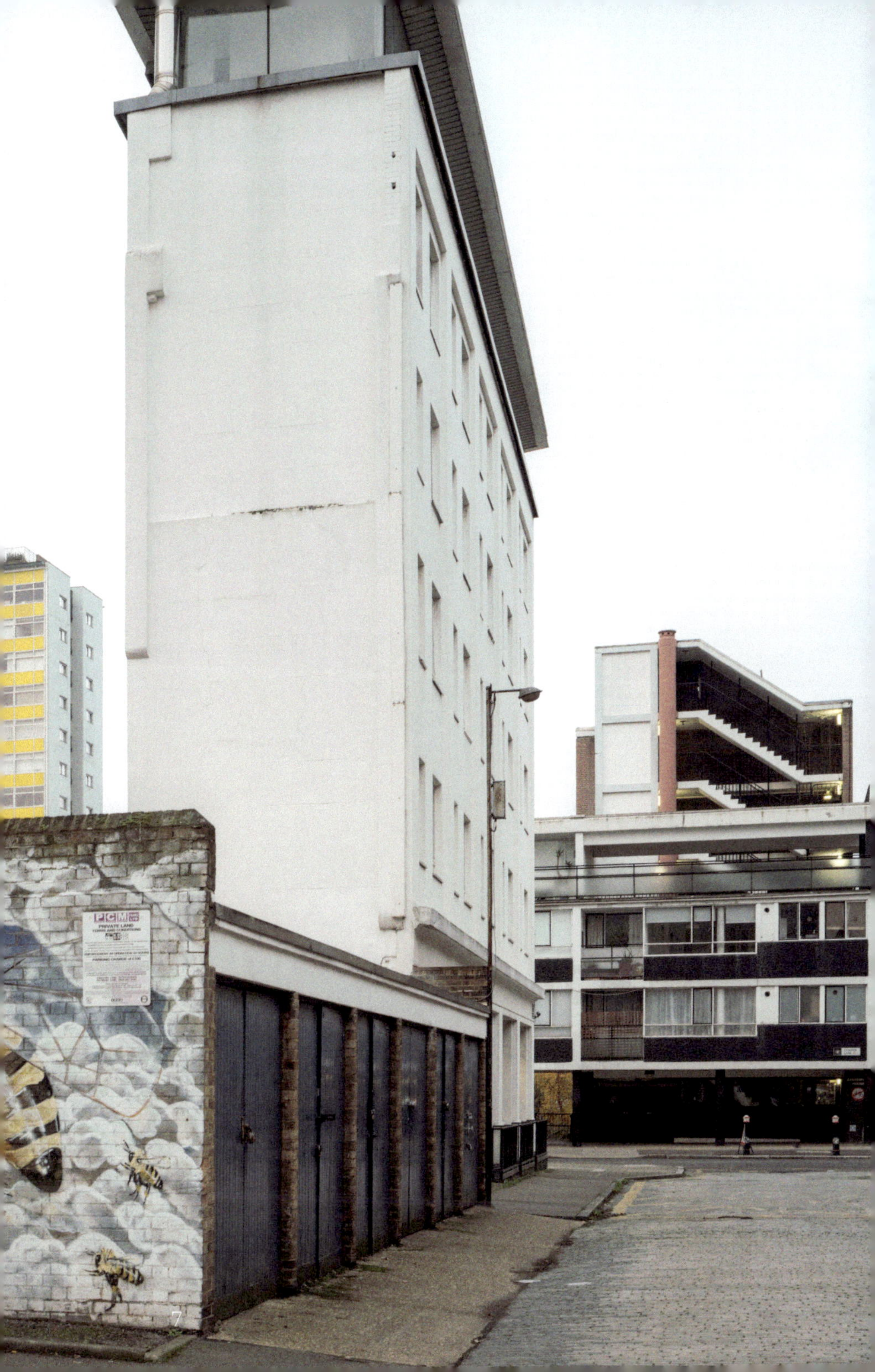
PCM
PRIVATE LAND

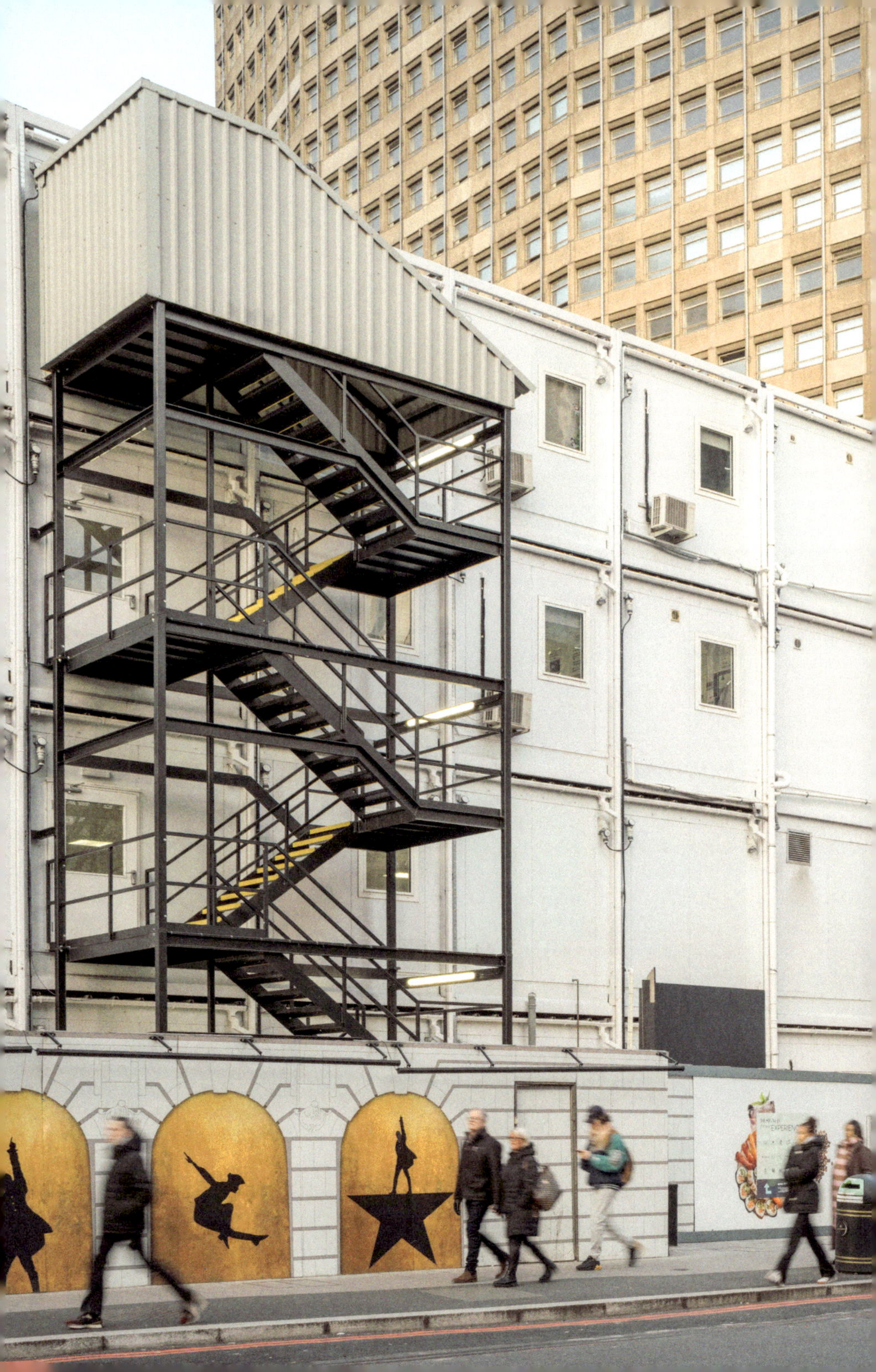

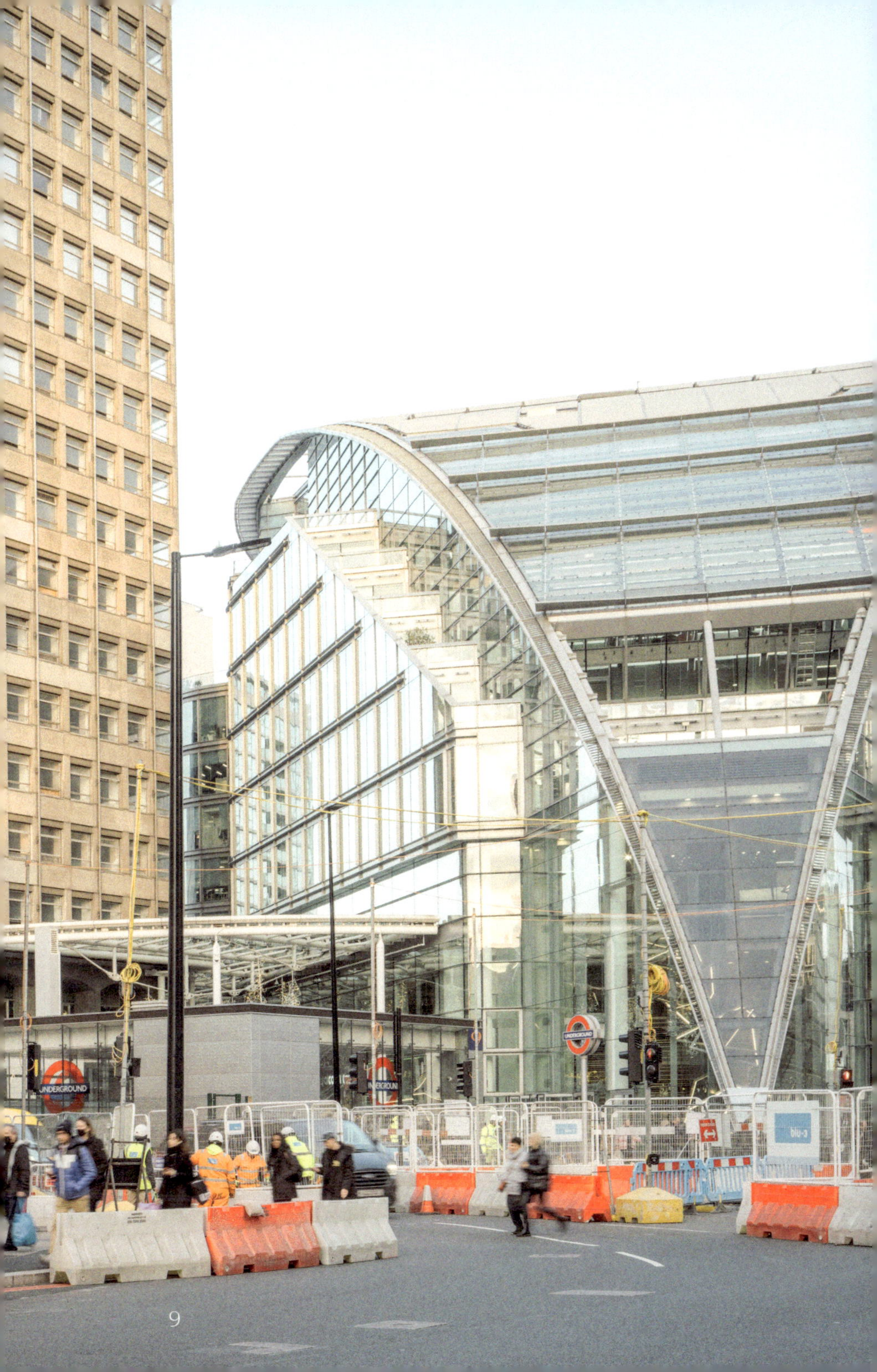
UNDERGROUND
UNDERGROUND

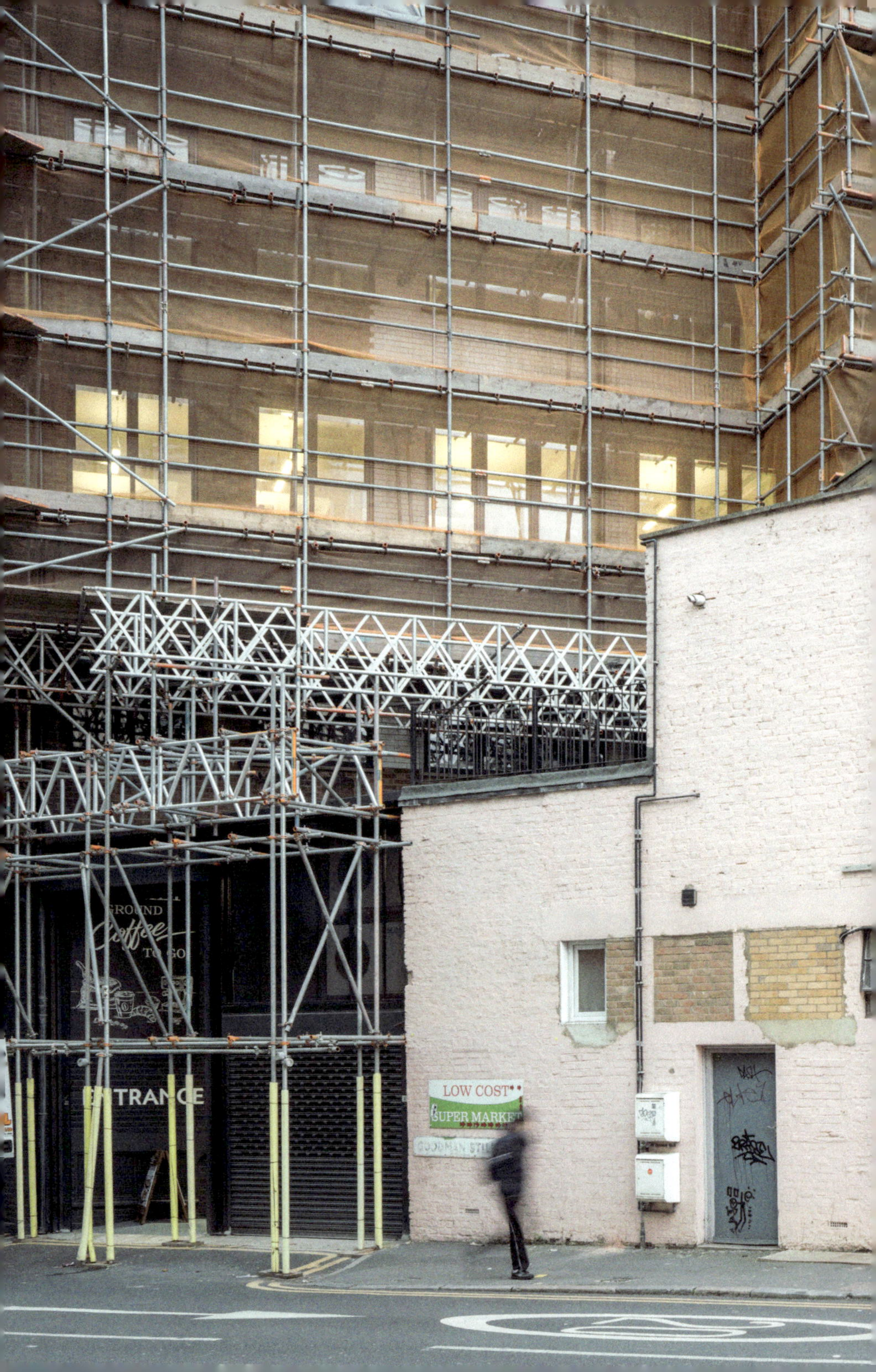
GROUND
Coffee
TO GO
TRANCE
LOW COST
SUPER MARKET

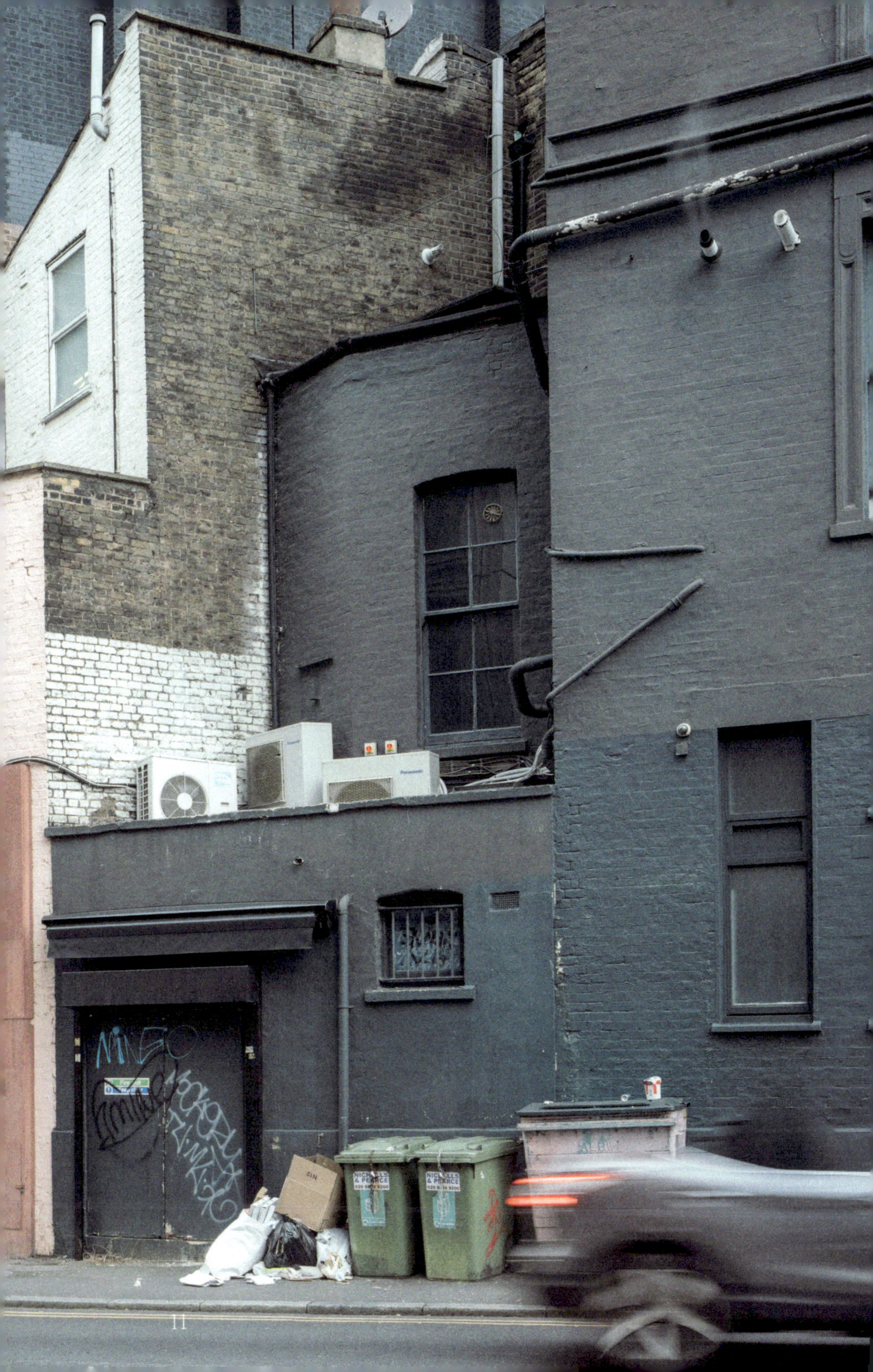

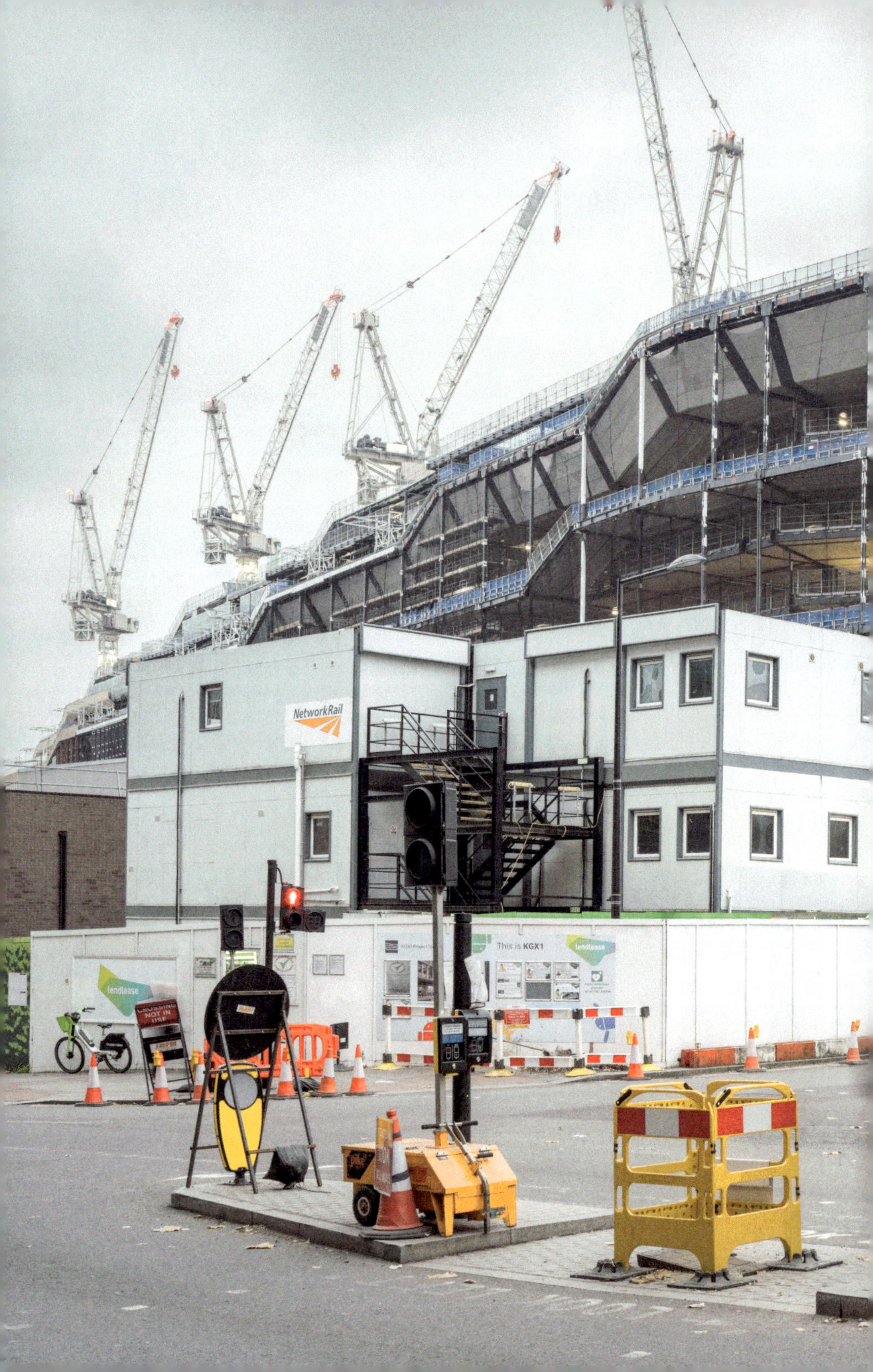
NetworkRail
lendlease
CROSSING NOT IN USE
This is KGX1
lendlease

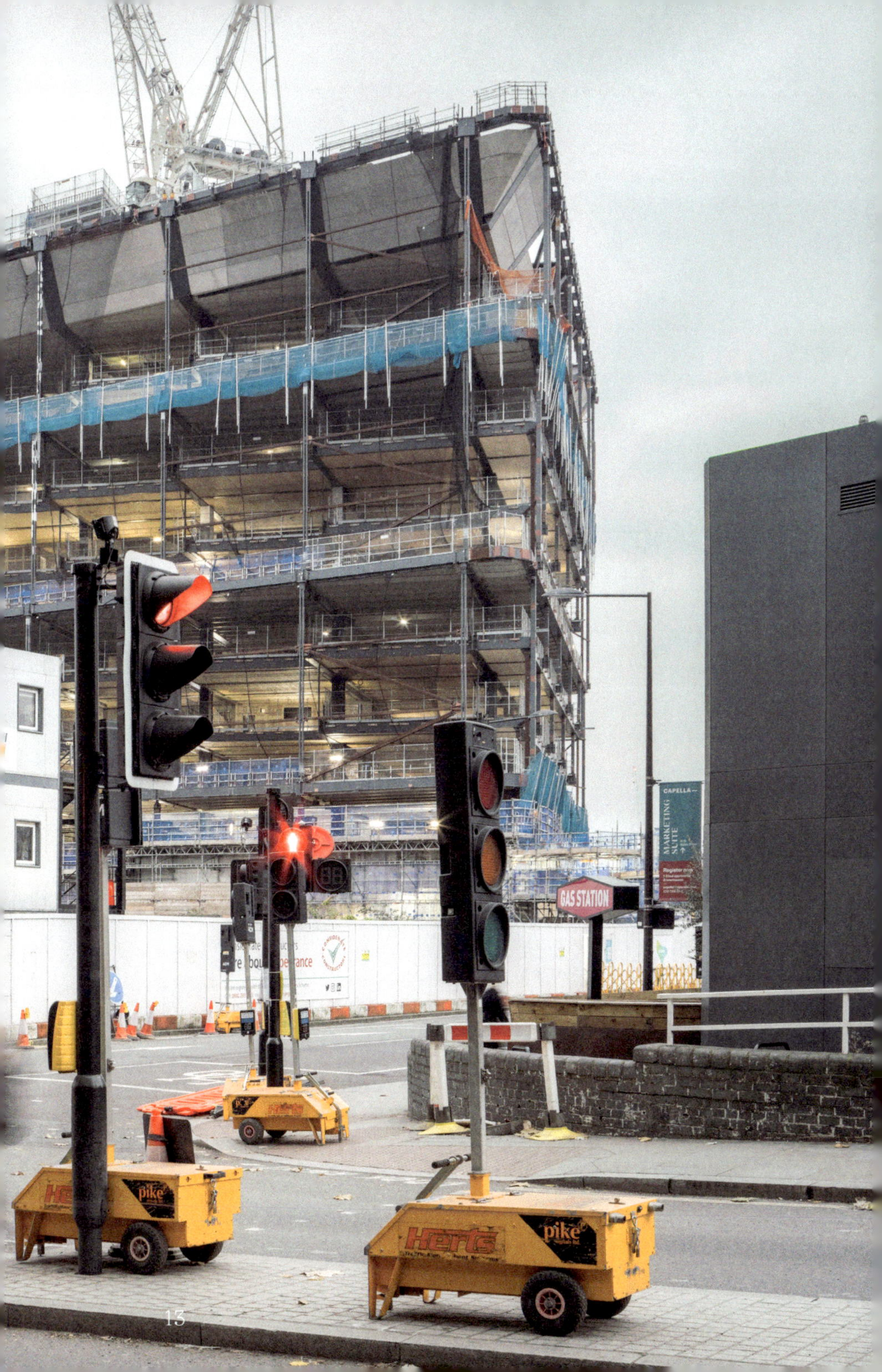
CAPELLA
MARKETING SUITE
GAS STATION
Herts
pike
Herts
pike

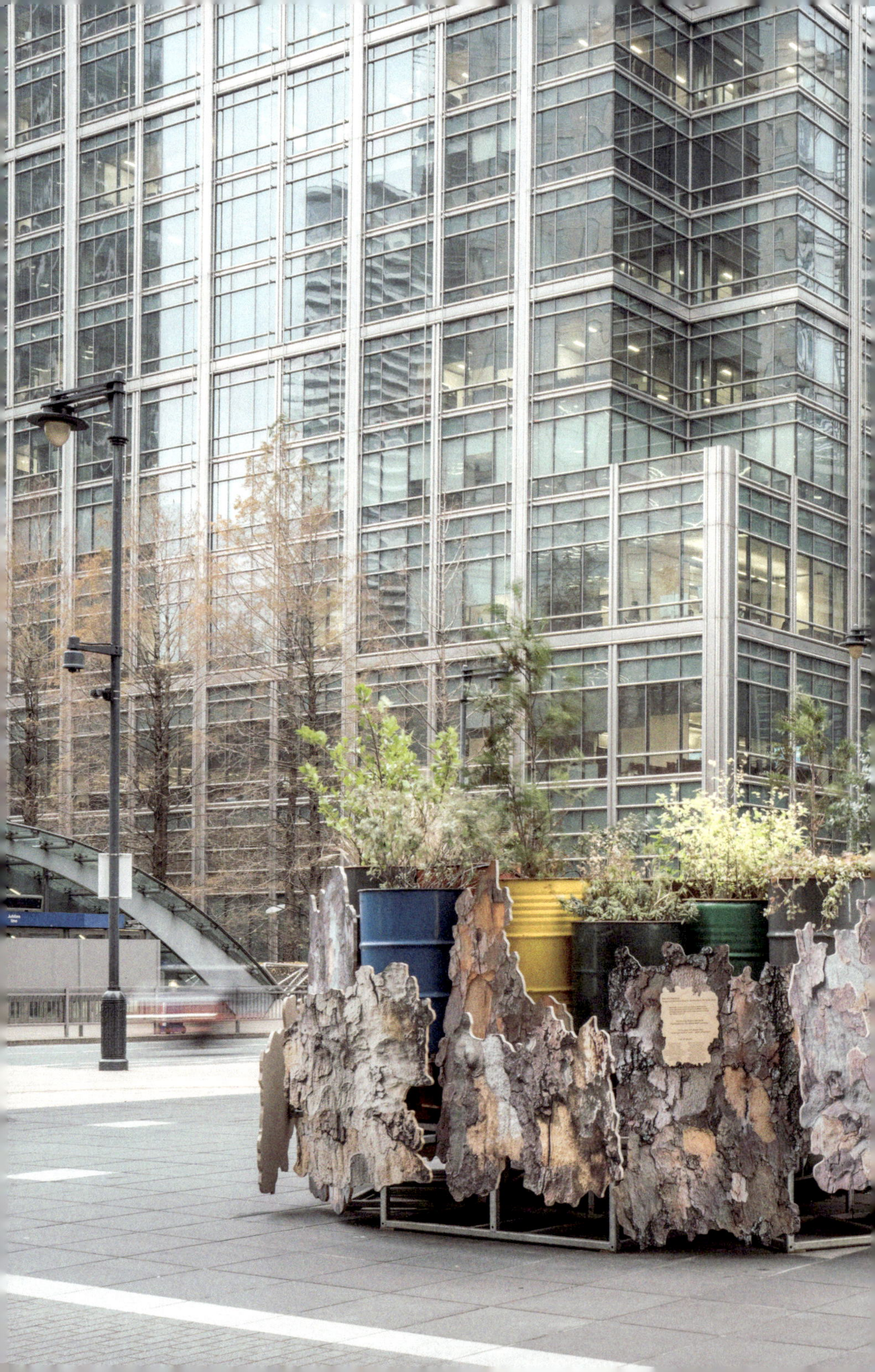

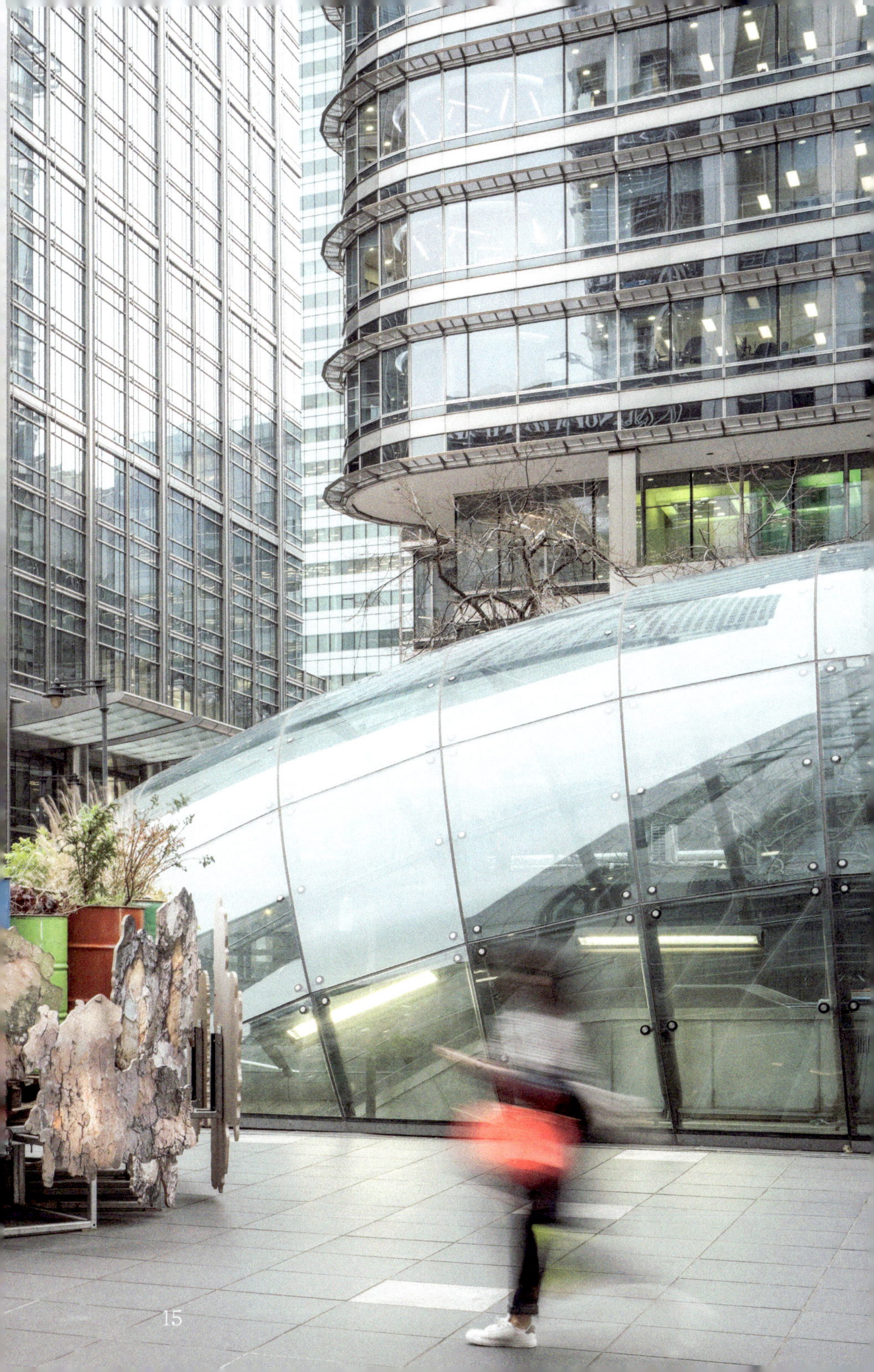

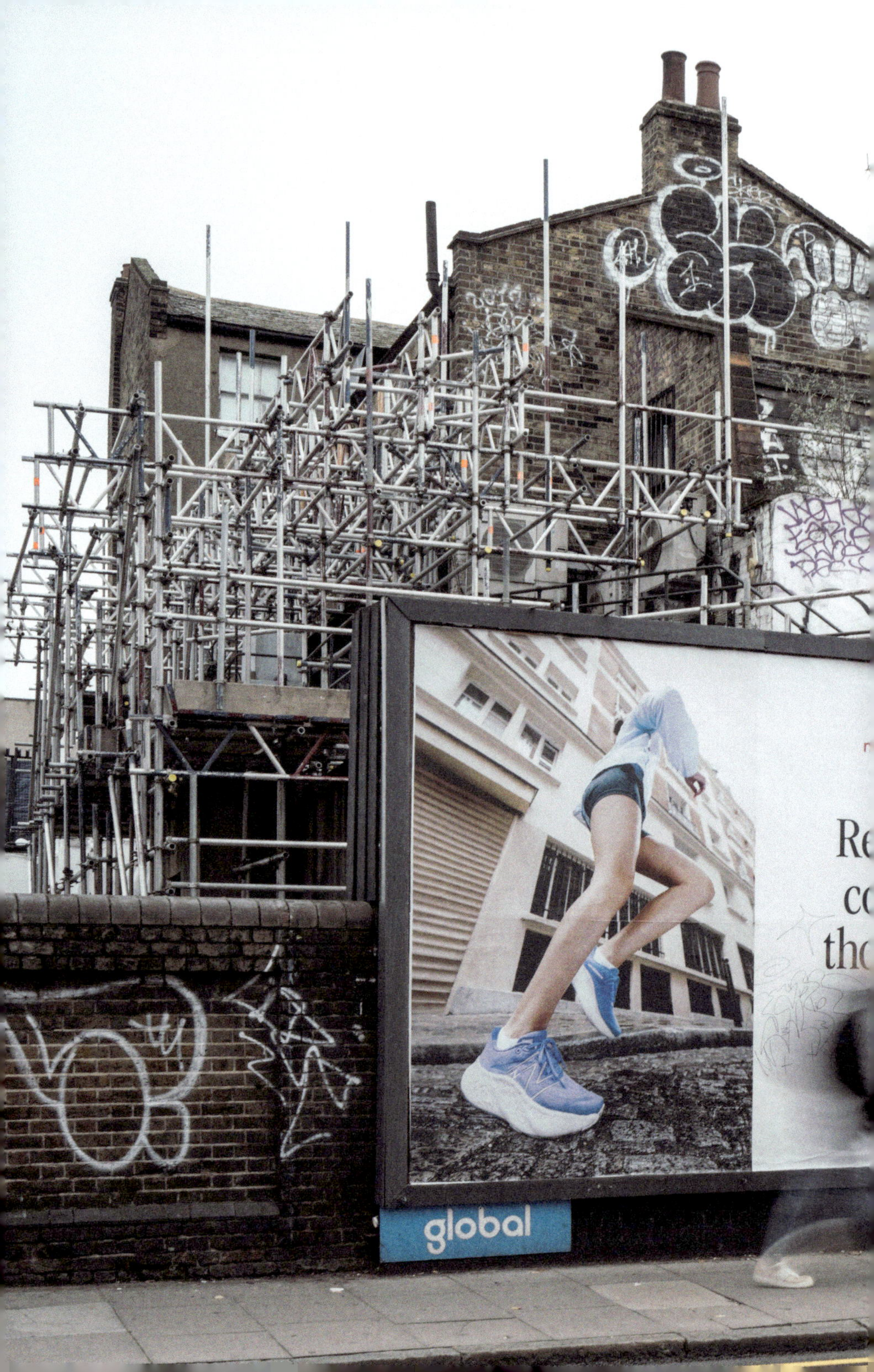
global

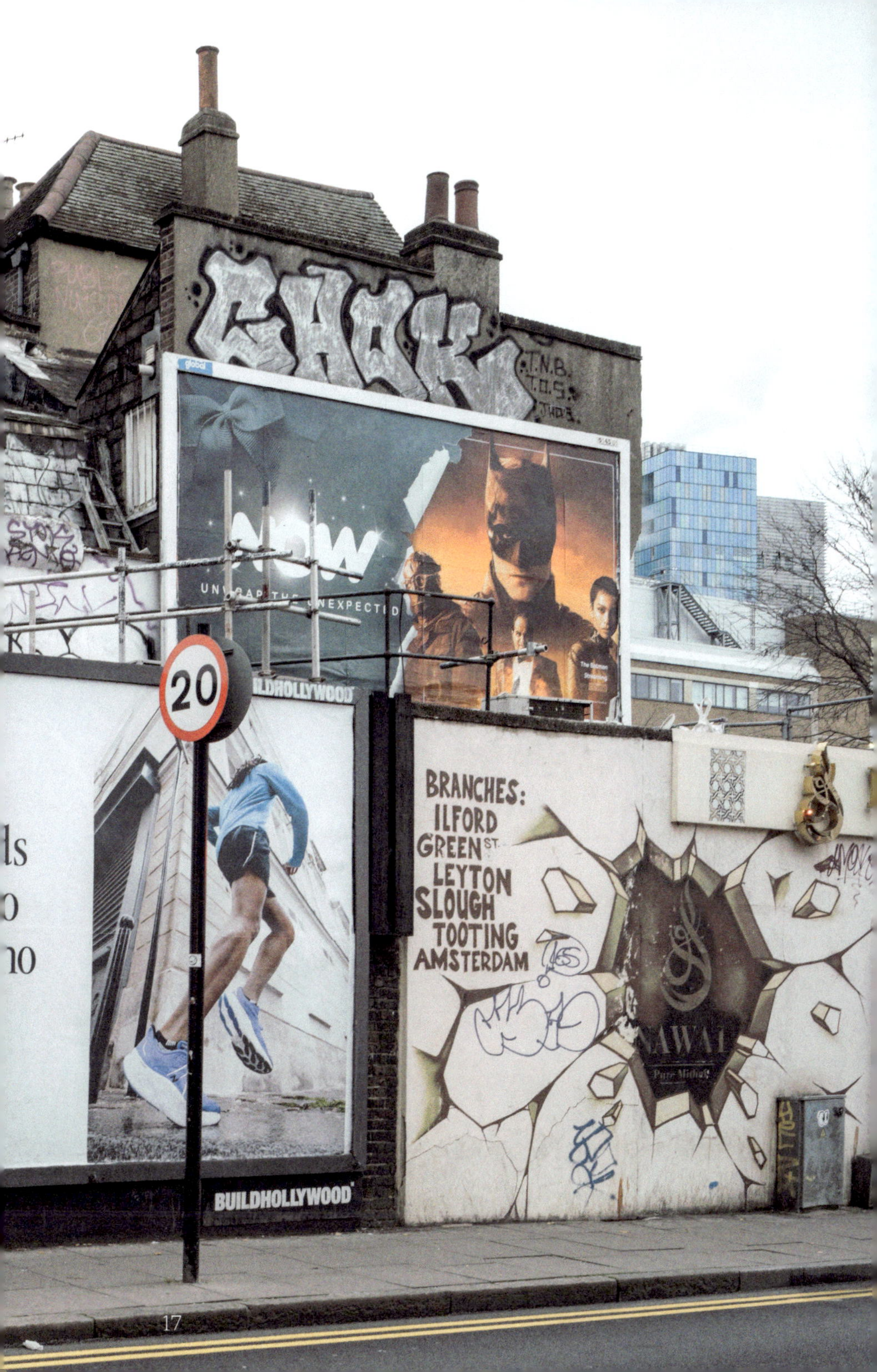
20
BUILDHOLLYWOOD
BUILDHOLLYWOOD
BRANCHES:
ILFORD
GREEN ST.
LEYTON
SLOUGH
TOOTING
AMSTERDAM
NAWAL

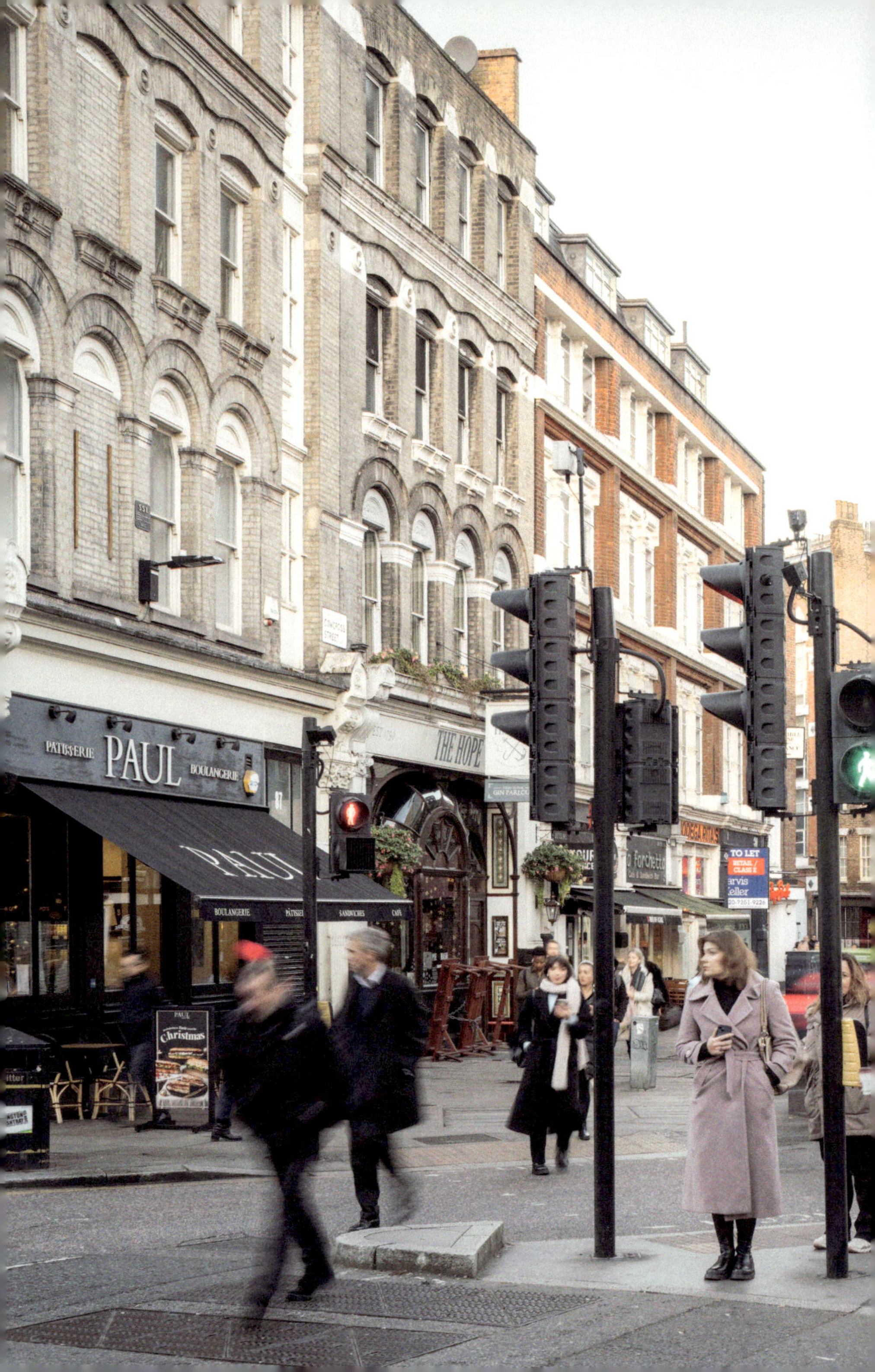
PATISSERIE
PAUL
BOULANGERIE
THE HOPE
PAUL
BOULANGERIE
SANDWICHES
CAFÉ
Christmas
TO LET

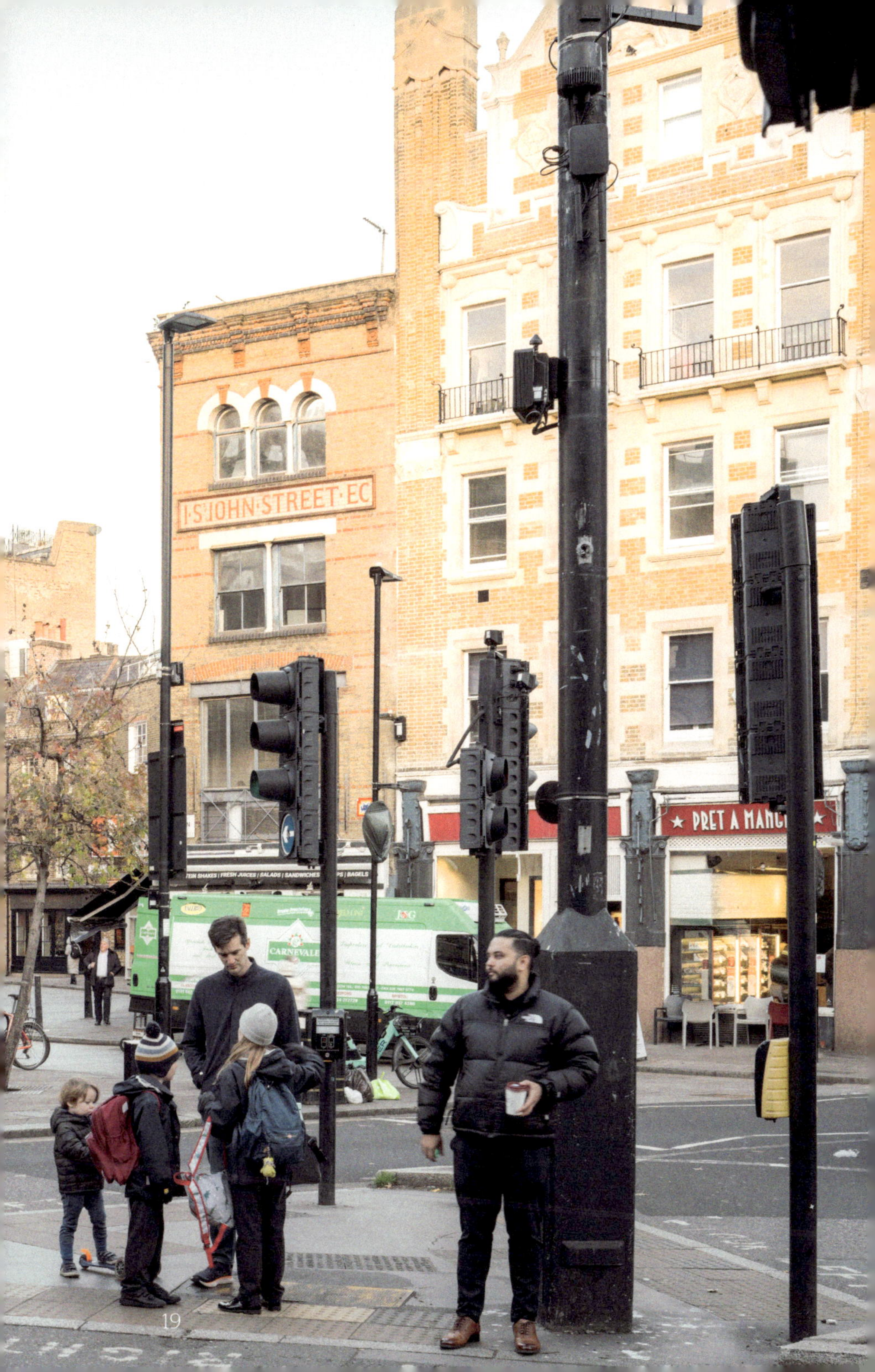
1·S·JOHN·STREET·EC
FRESH JUICES | SALADS | SANDWICHES
CARNEVALE
PRET A MANG

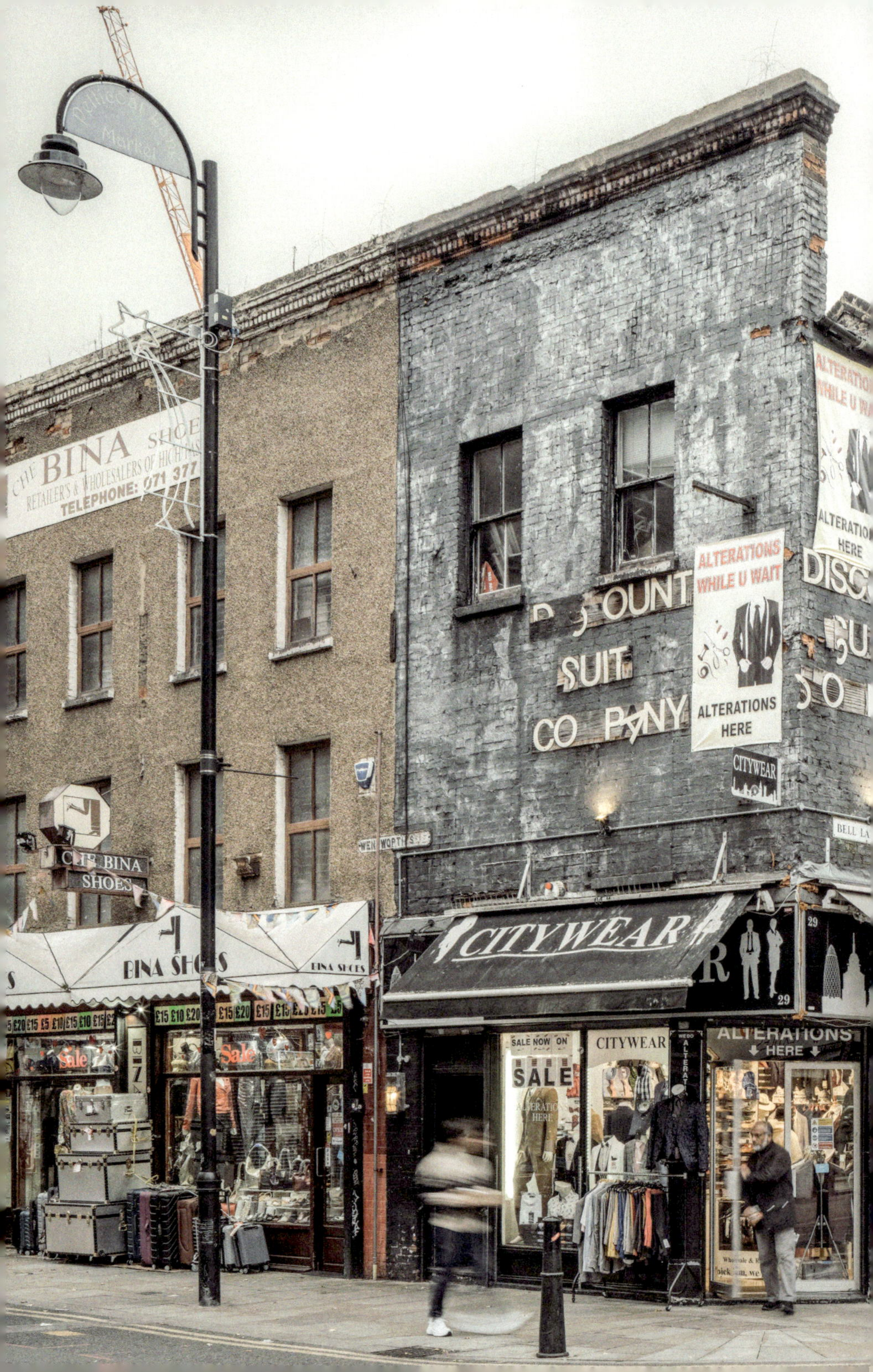

TELEPHONE: 071 377
CHE BINA
SHOES
BINA SHOES
BINA SHOES
Sale
Sale
SUIT
ALTERATIONS
WHILE U WAIT
ALTERATIONS
HERE
CITYWEAR
CITYWEAR
SALE NOW ON
SALE
CITYWEAR
ALTERATIONS
HERE

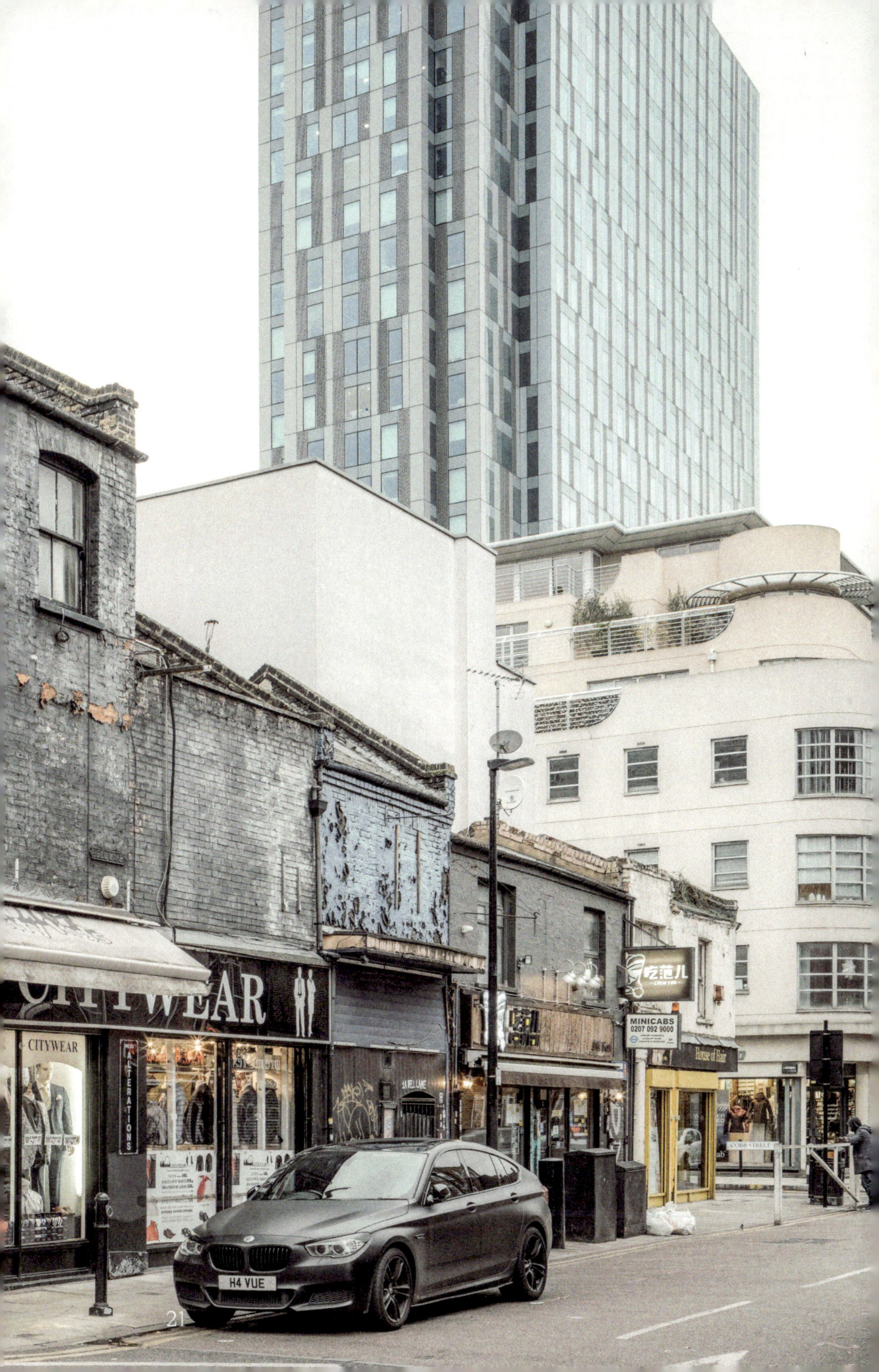
CITYWEAR
CITYWEAR
ALTERATIONS
吃范儿
MINICABS
0207 092 9000
House of Hair
COBB STREET
H4 VUE

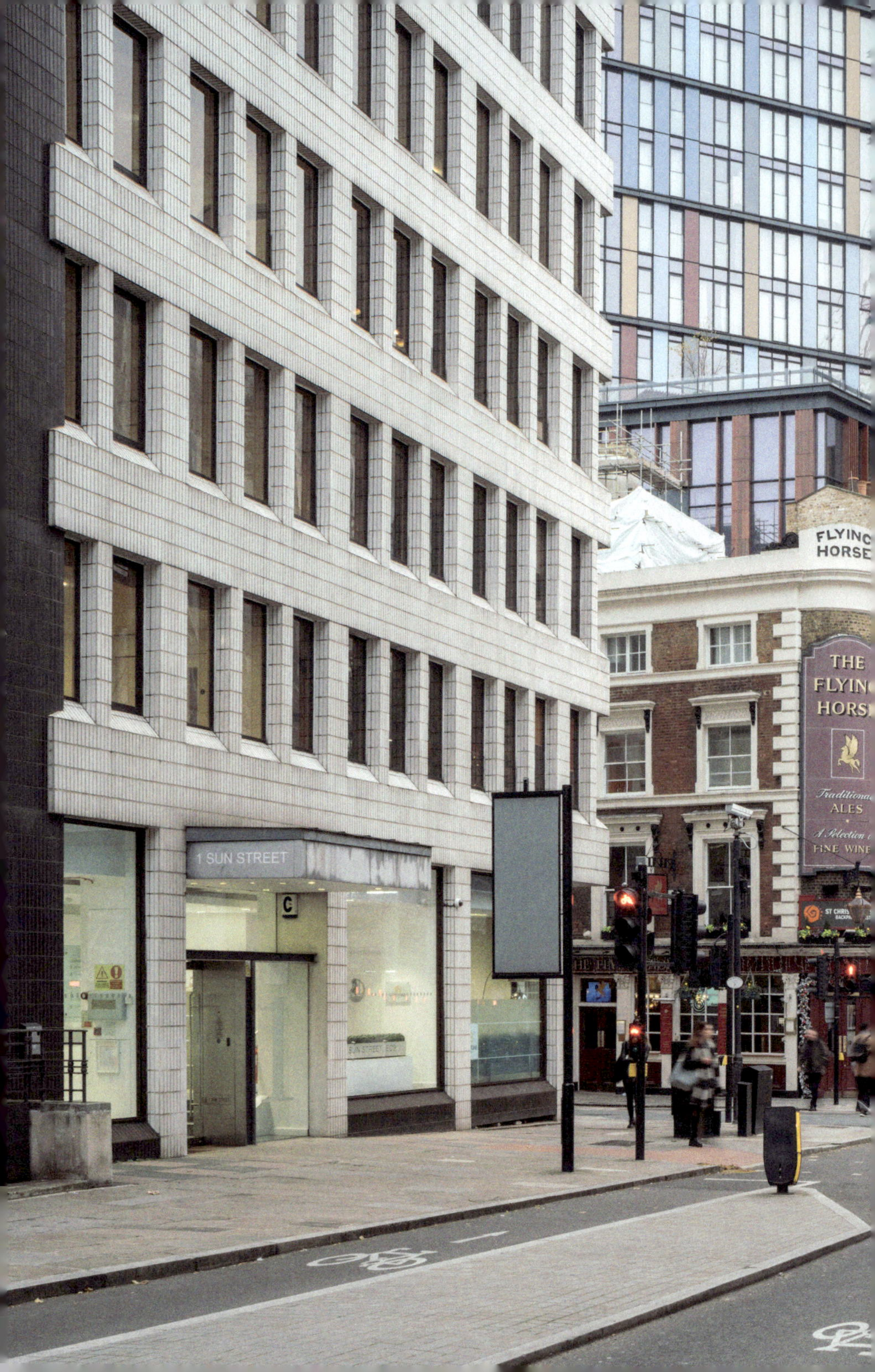
1 SUN STREET
C
FLYING
HORSE
THE
FLYING
HORS
Traditional
ALES
A Selection of
FINE WINE

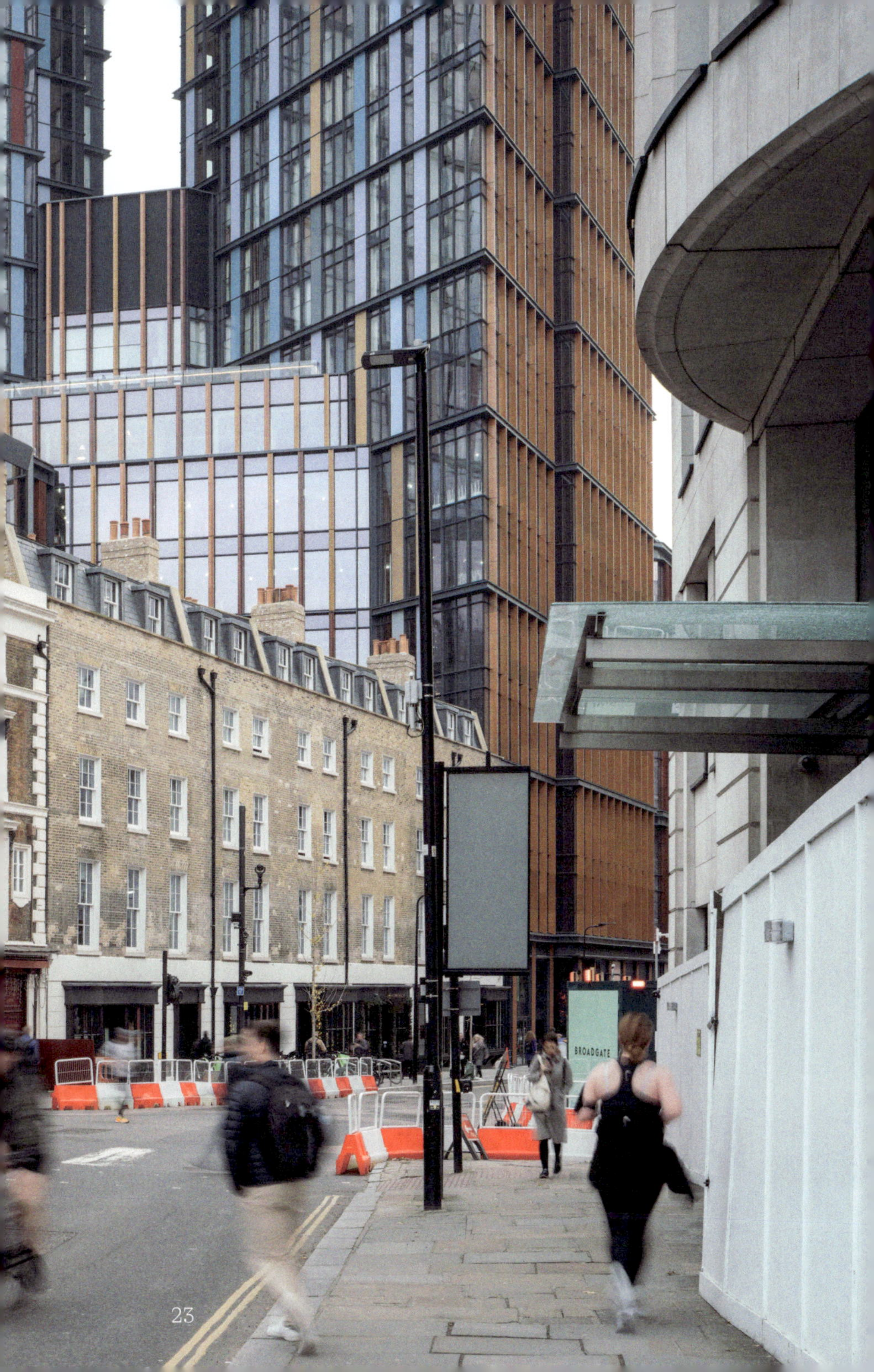
BROADGATE

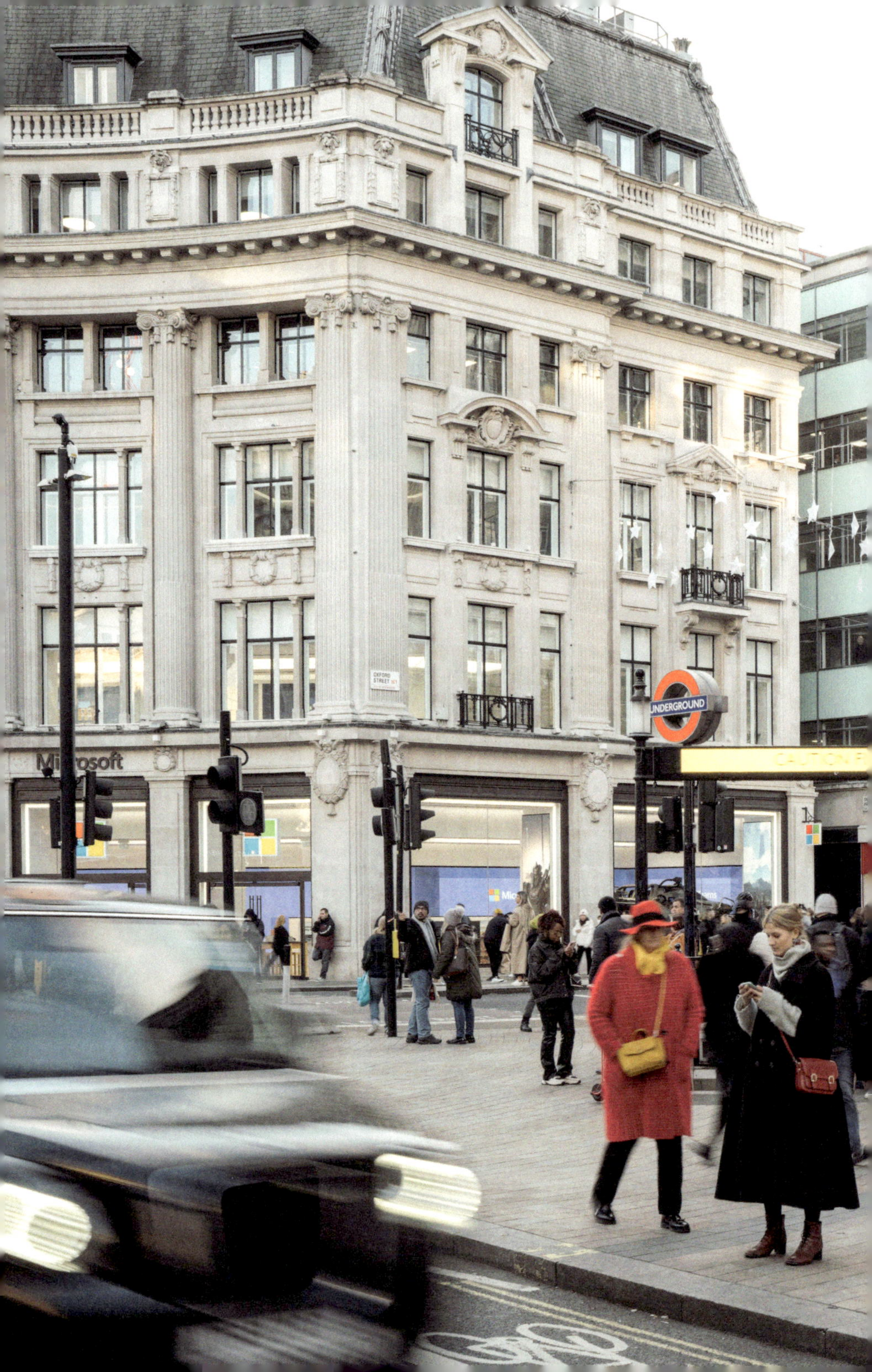
OXFORD
STREET W1
Microsoft
UNDERGROUND

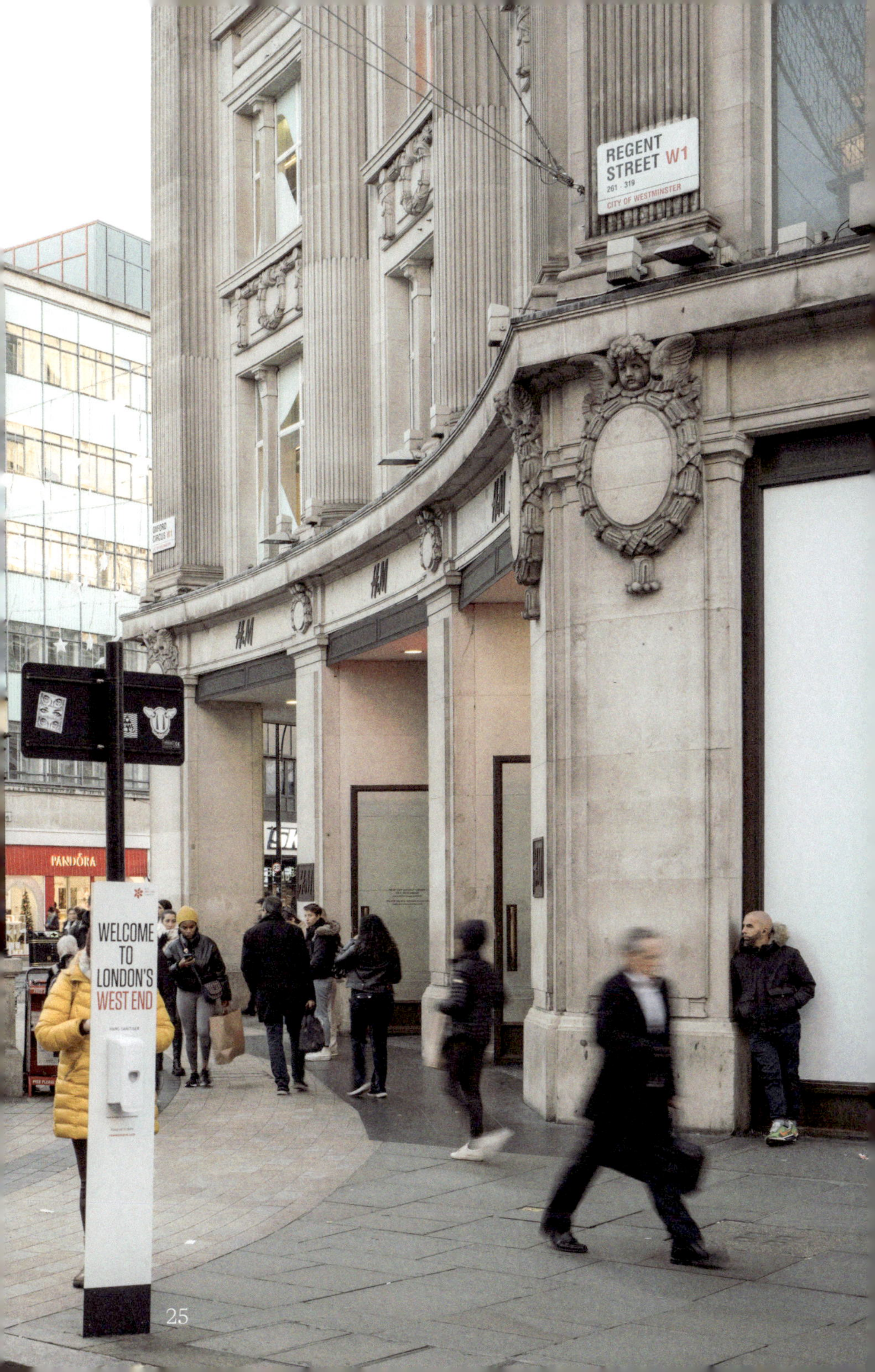
REGENT
STREET W1
261 - 319
CITY OF WESTMINSTER
H&M
PANDORA
WELCOME
TO
LONDON'S
WEST END

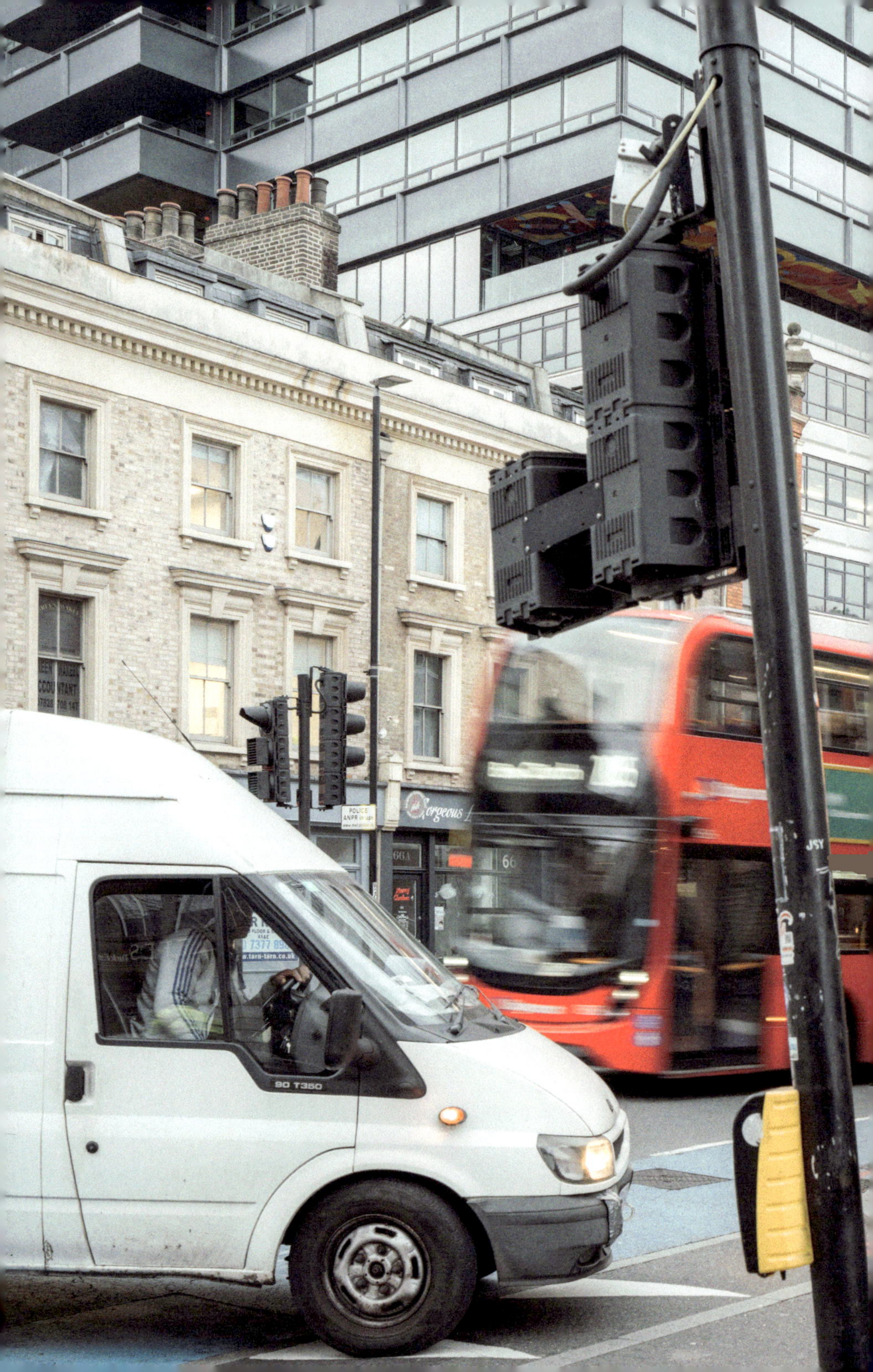
ACCOUNTANT
POLICE
ANPR in use
66A
90 T350
JSY

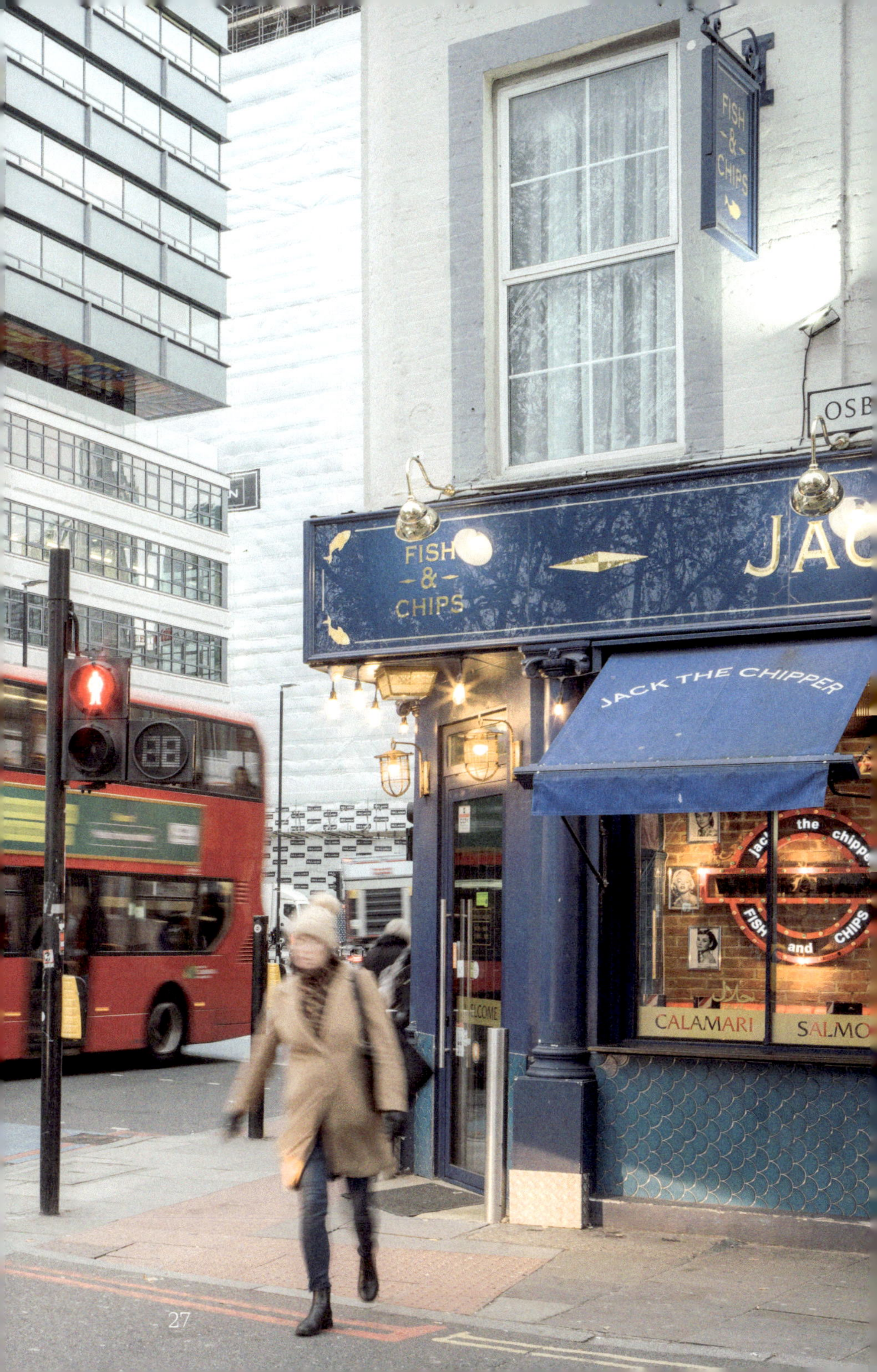
FISH & CHIPS
OSB
FISH & CHIPS
JAC
JACK THE CHIPPER
Jack the chipper
FISH and CHIPS
CALAMARI
SALMO

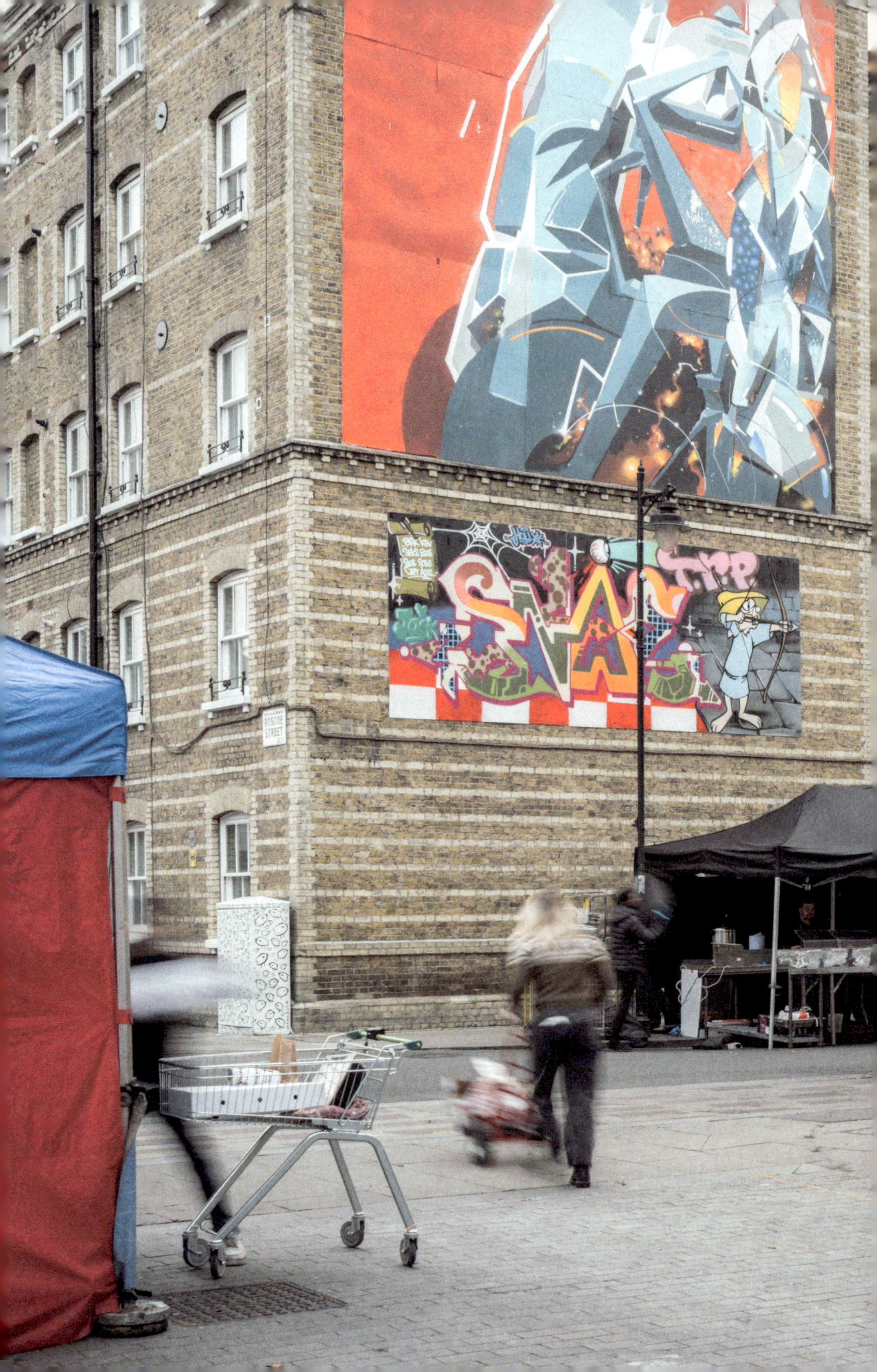
ROSCOE STREET

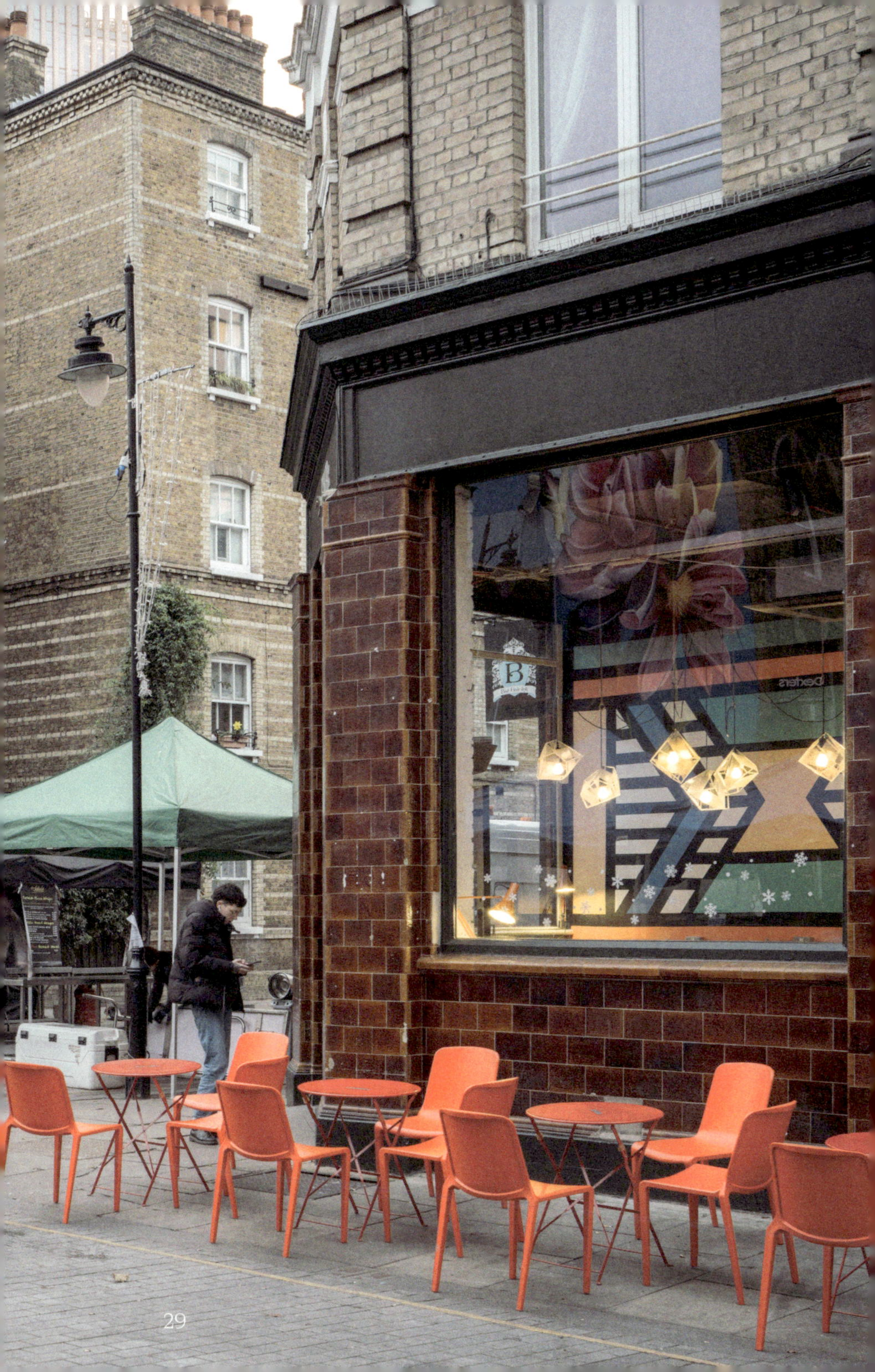

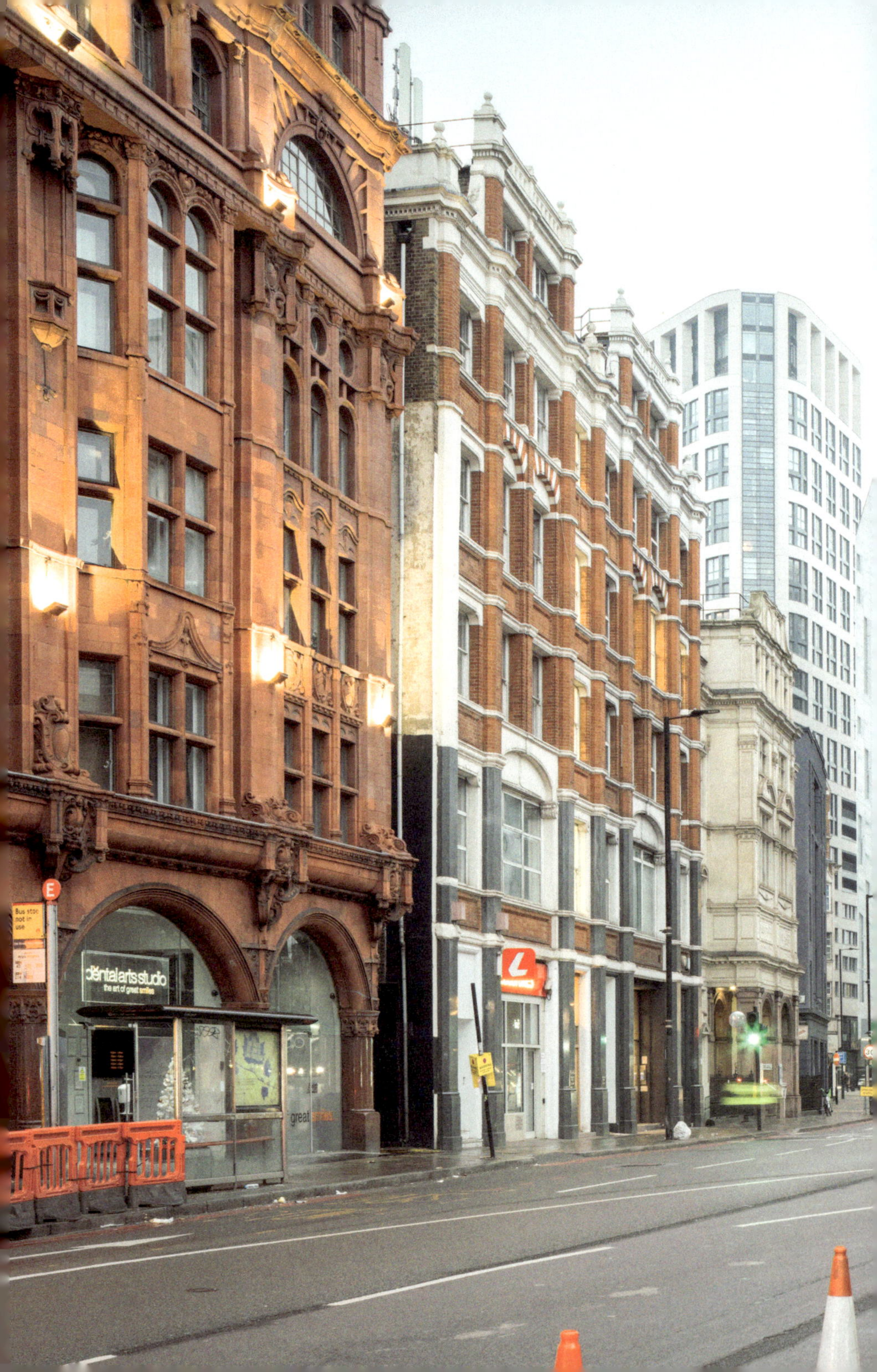
E
Bus stop not in use
dental arts studio
the art of great smiles
great smiles

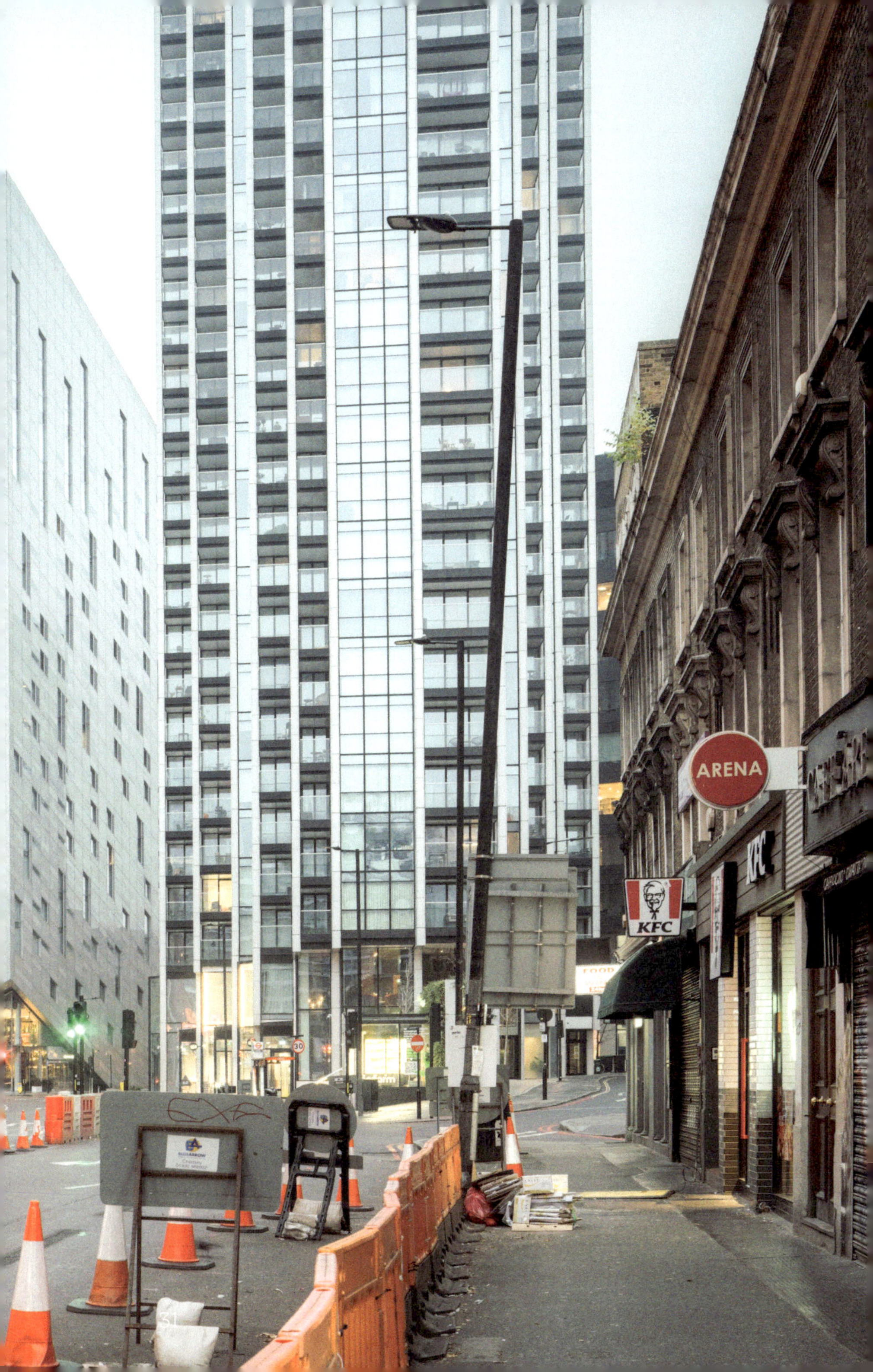
ARENA
KFC
KFC

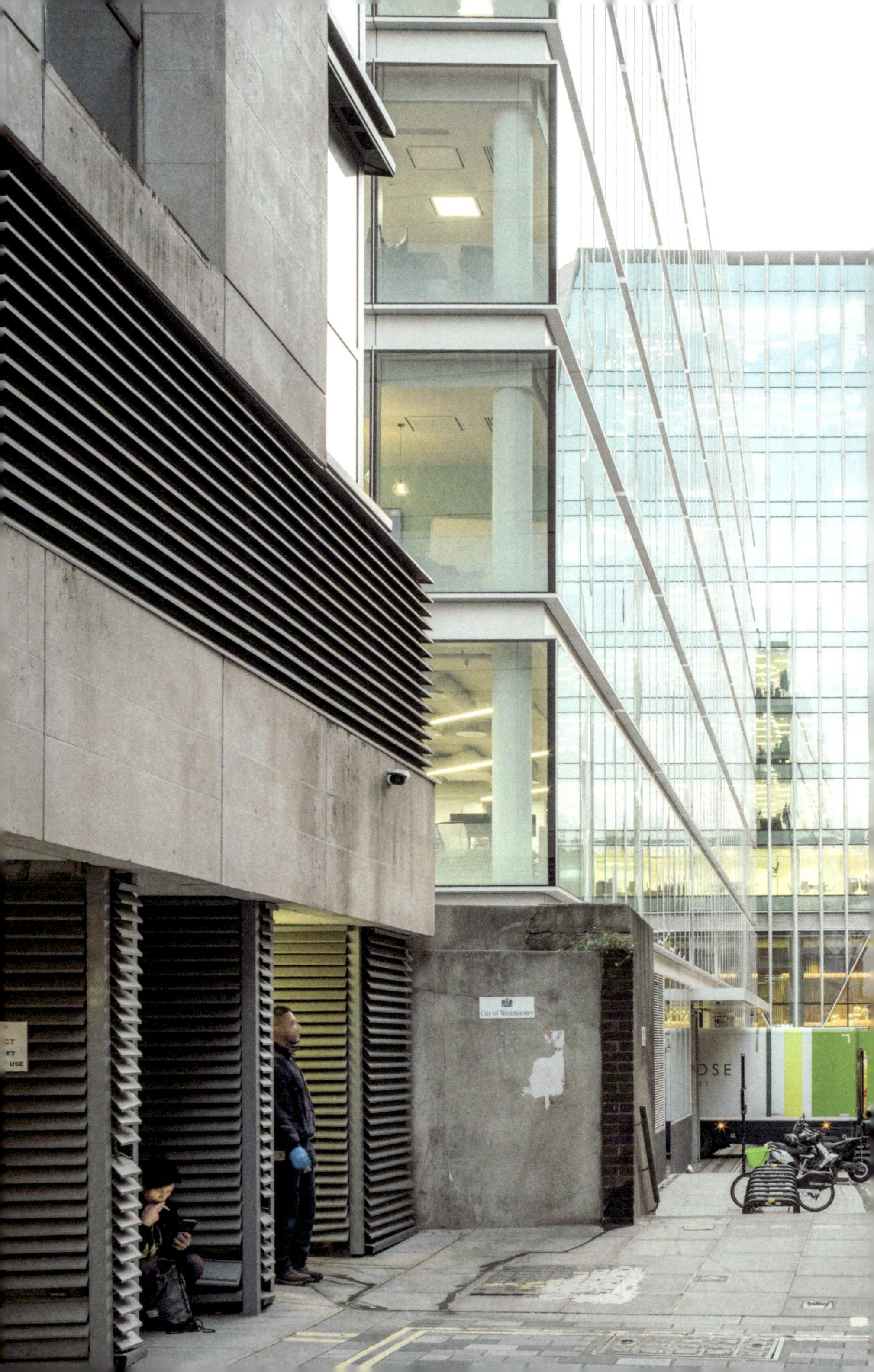
City of Westminster

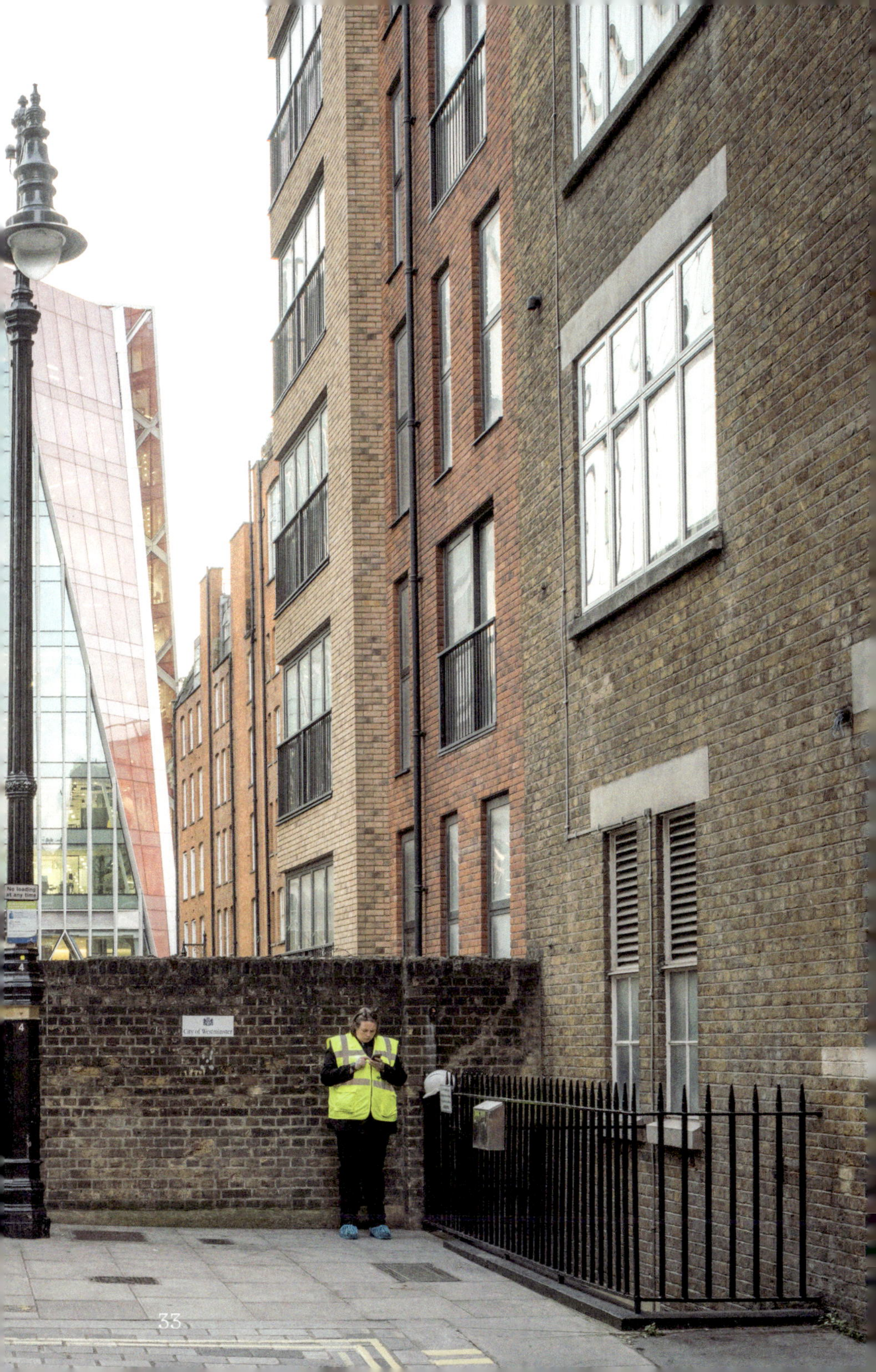
No loading
at any time
4
4
City of Westminster

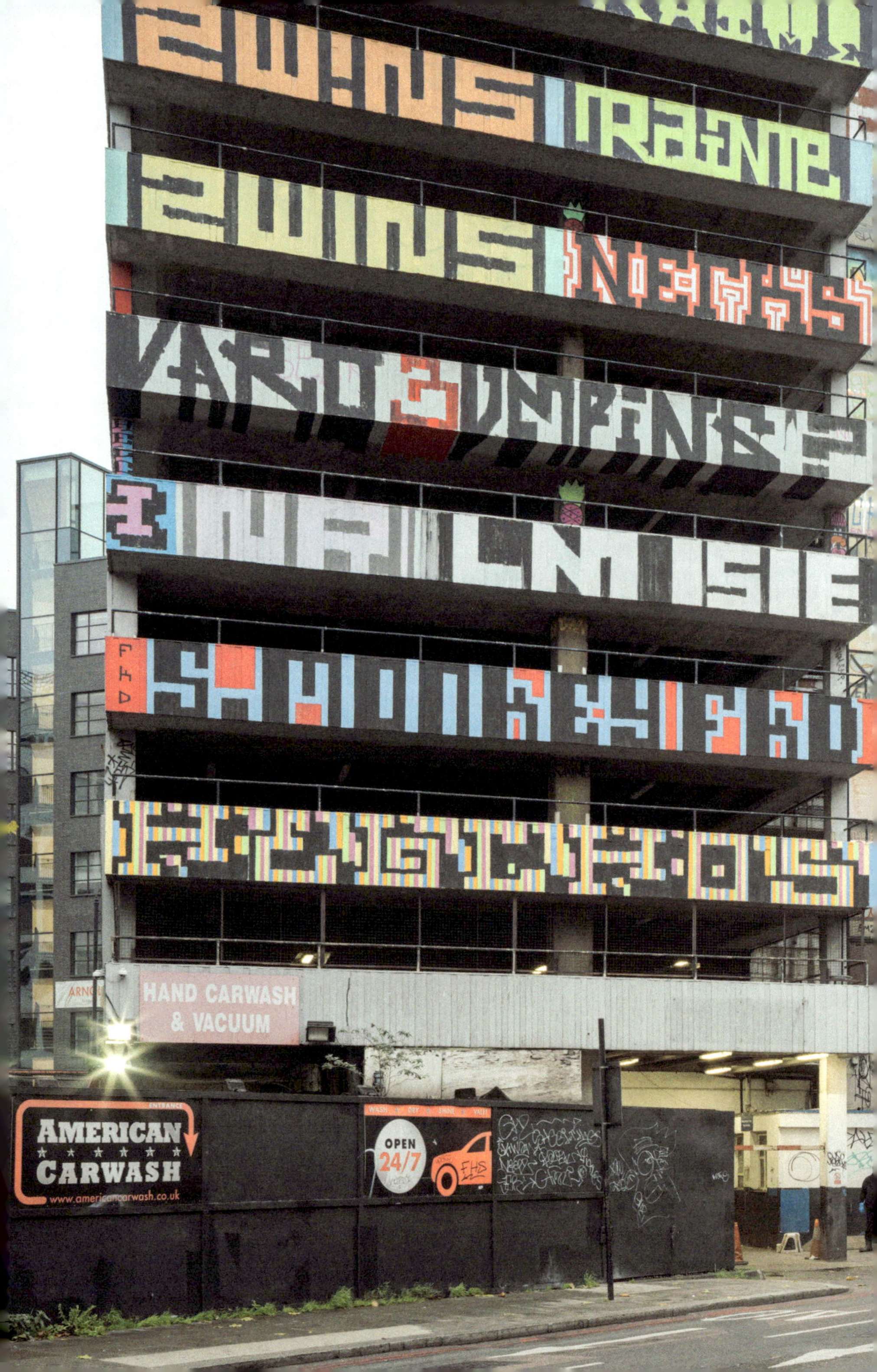
HAND CARWASH
& VACUUM
ENTRANCE
AMERICAN
CARWASH
www.americancarwash.co.uk
WASH DRY SHINE VALET
OPEN
24/7

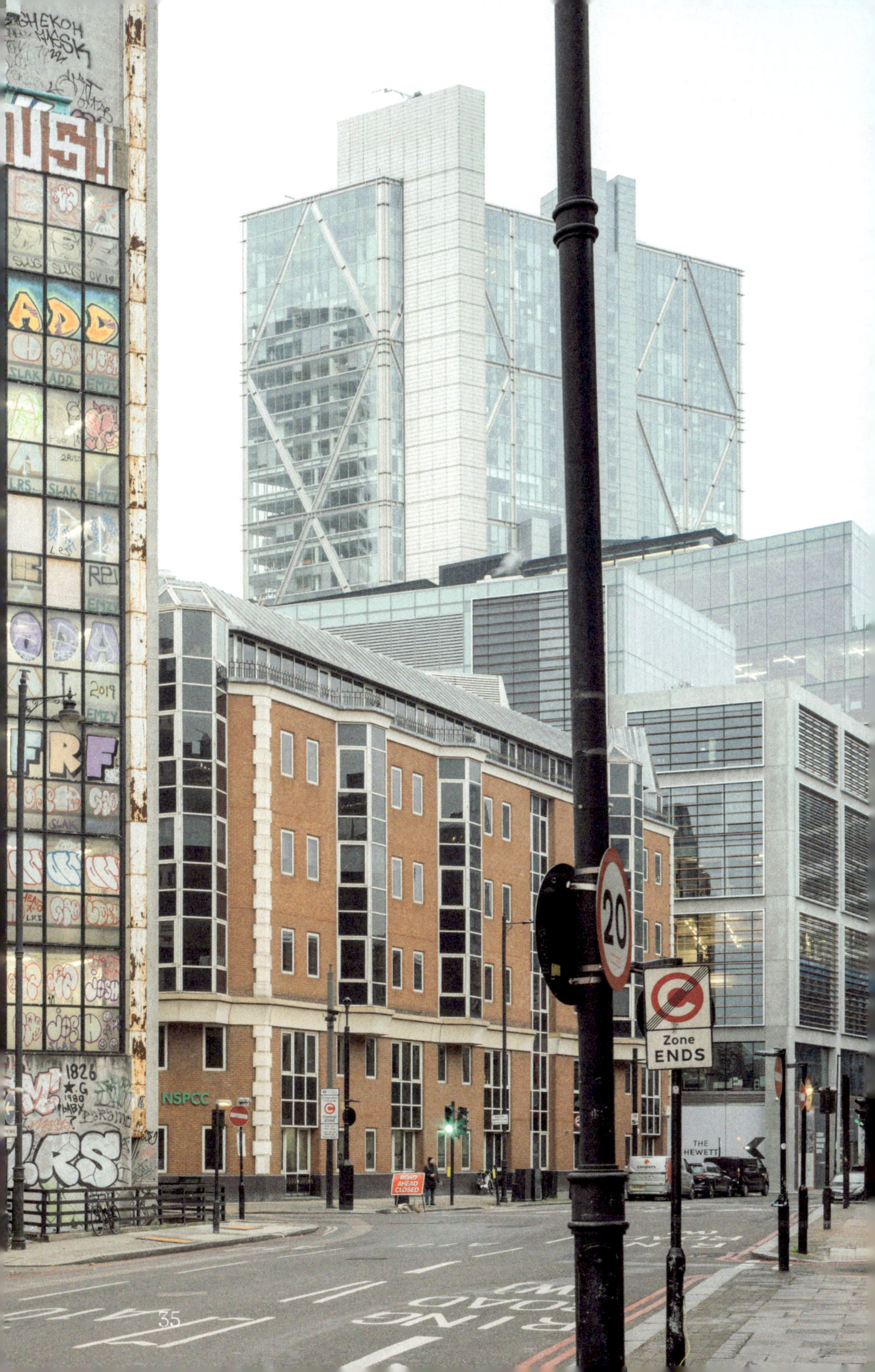
20
Zone
ENDS
NSPCC
ROAD
AHEAD
CLOSED
THE
HEWETT

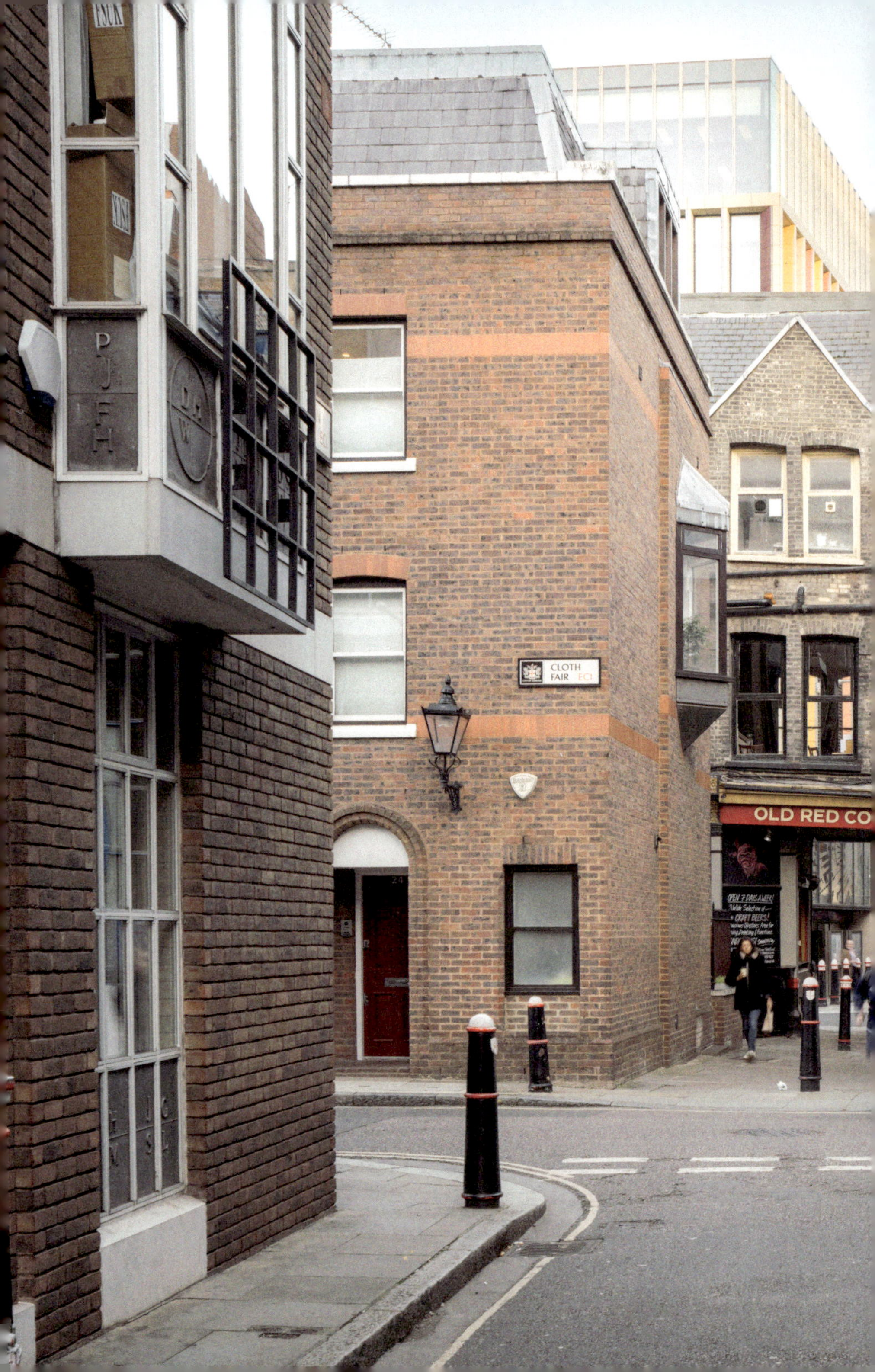
CLOTH
FAIR EC1
OLD RED CO
OPEN 7 DAYS A WEEK!
CRAFT BEERS!

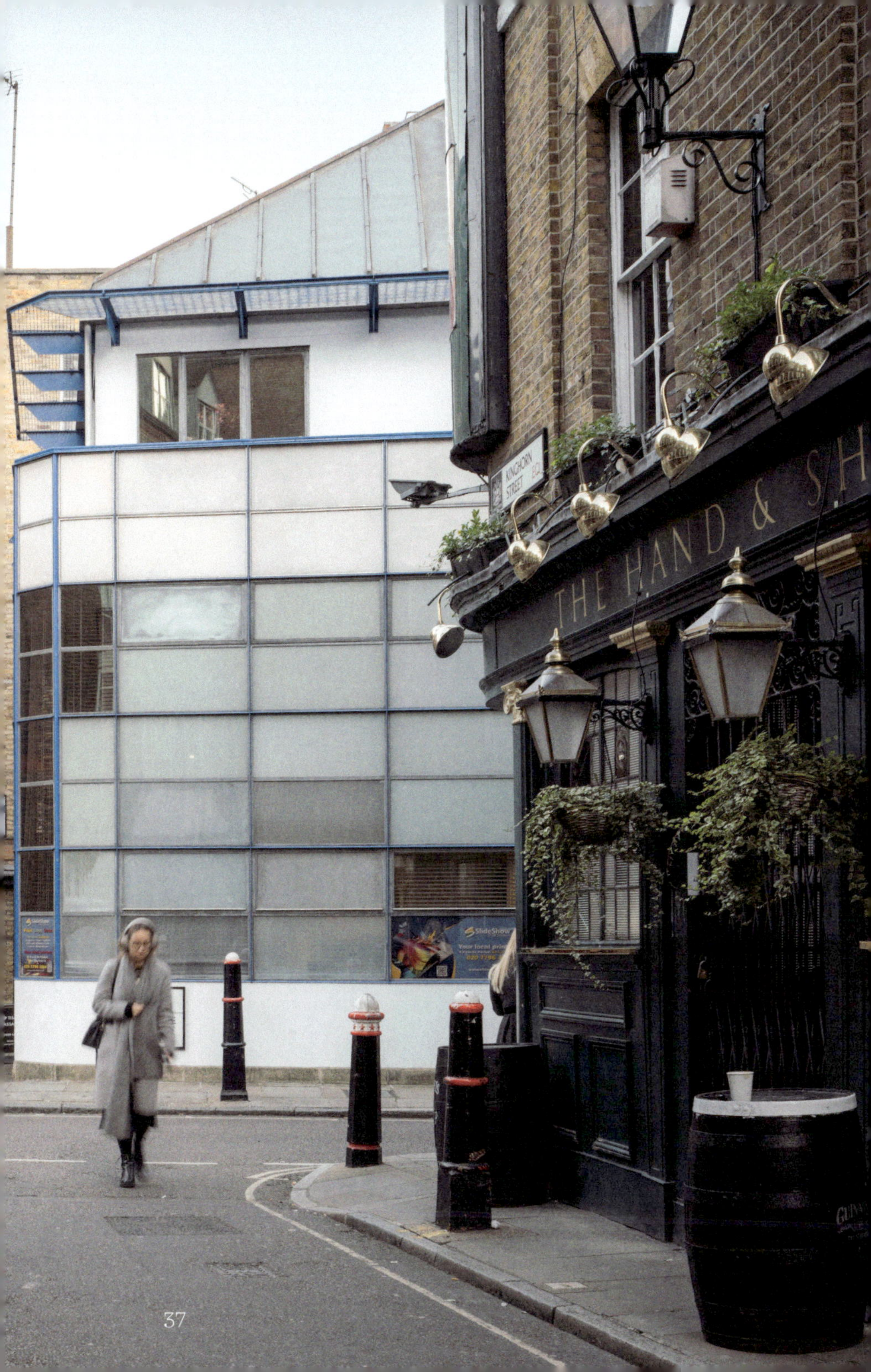
KINGHORN STREET EC1
THE HAND & SH
SlideShow

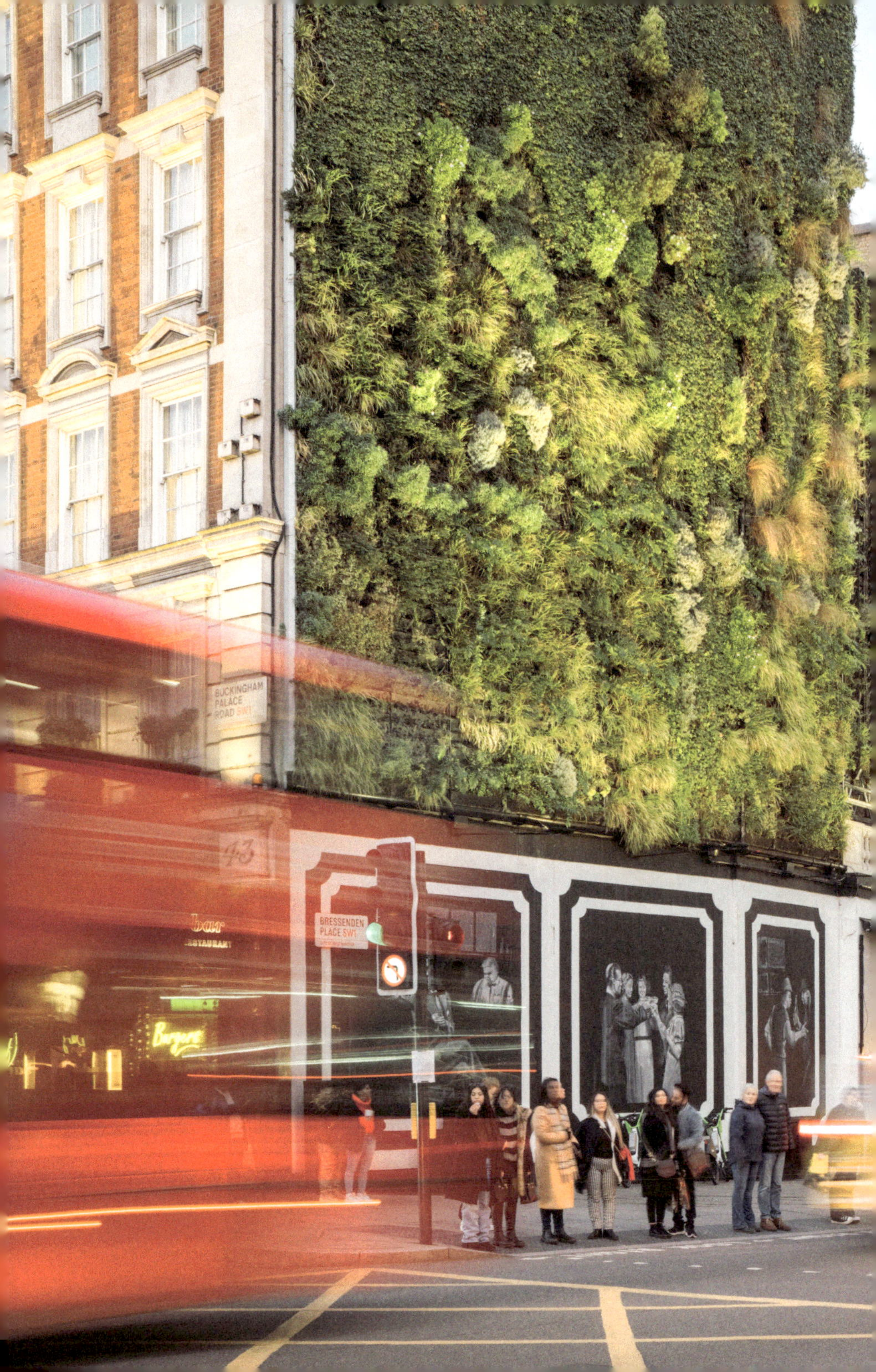
BUCKINGHAM PALACE ROAD SW1
43
bar
BRESSENDEN PLACE SW1

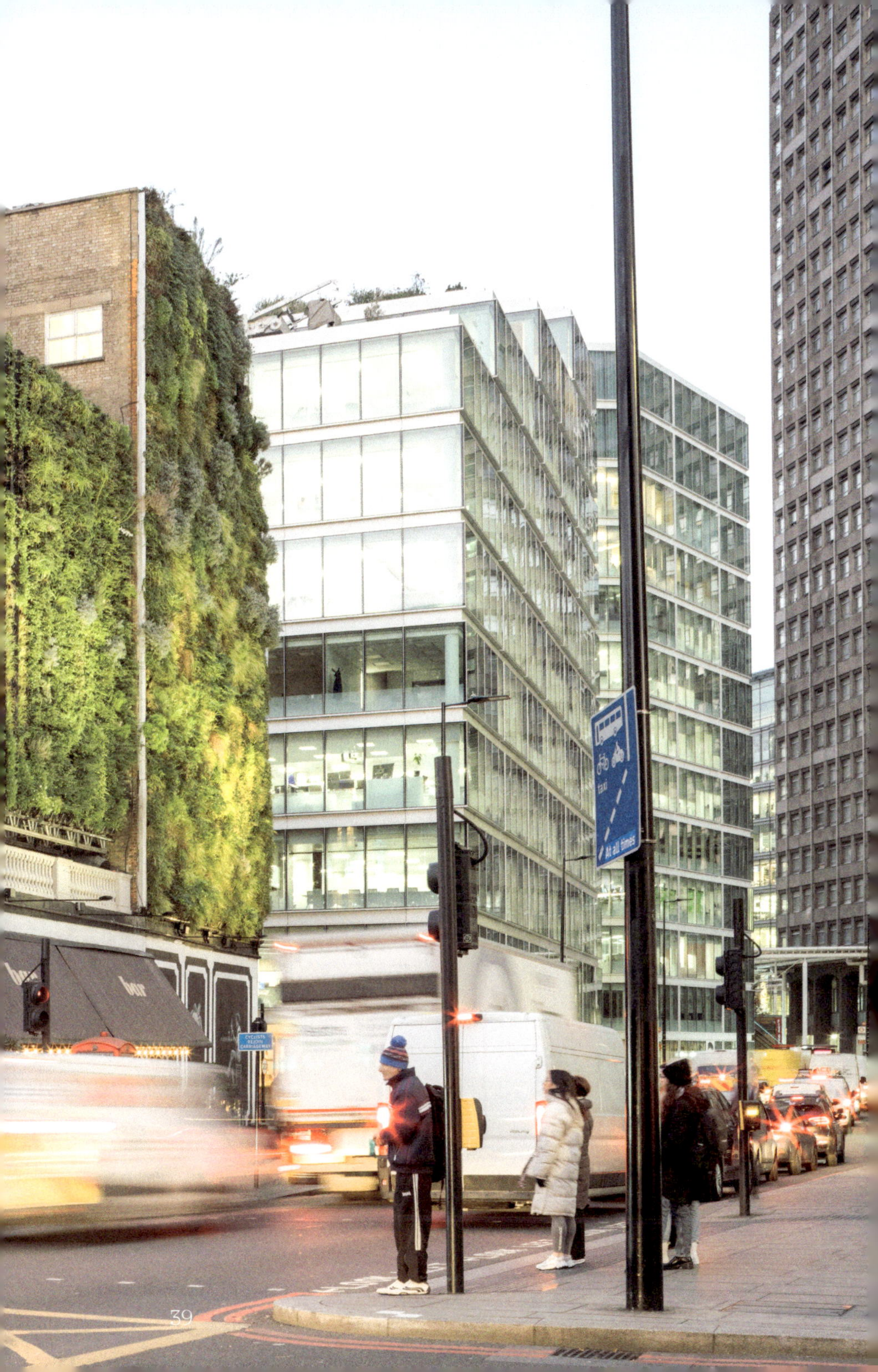
taxi
At all times
bar

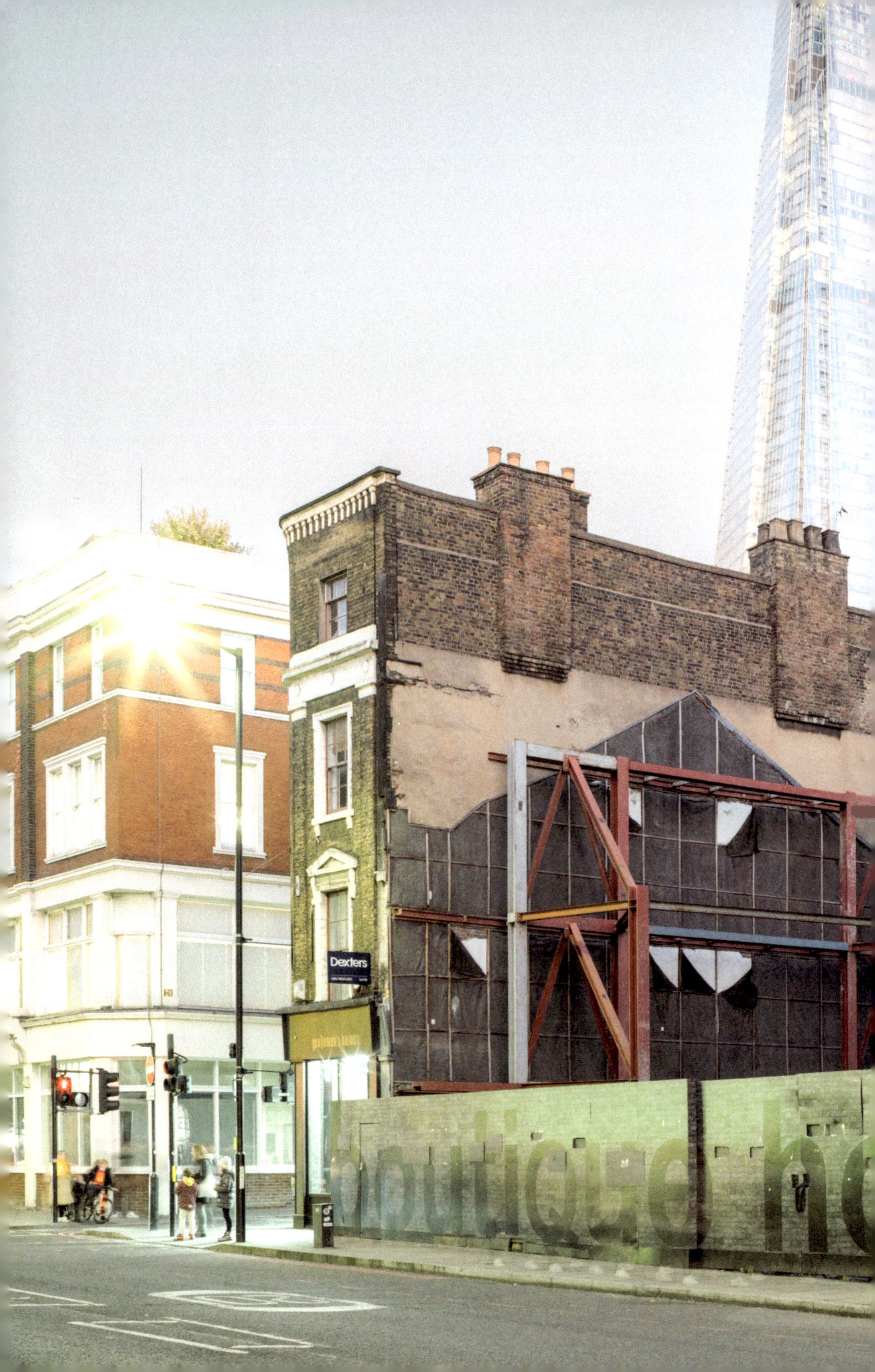
Dexters

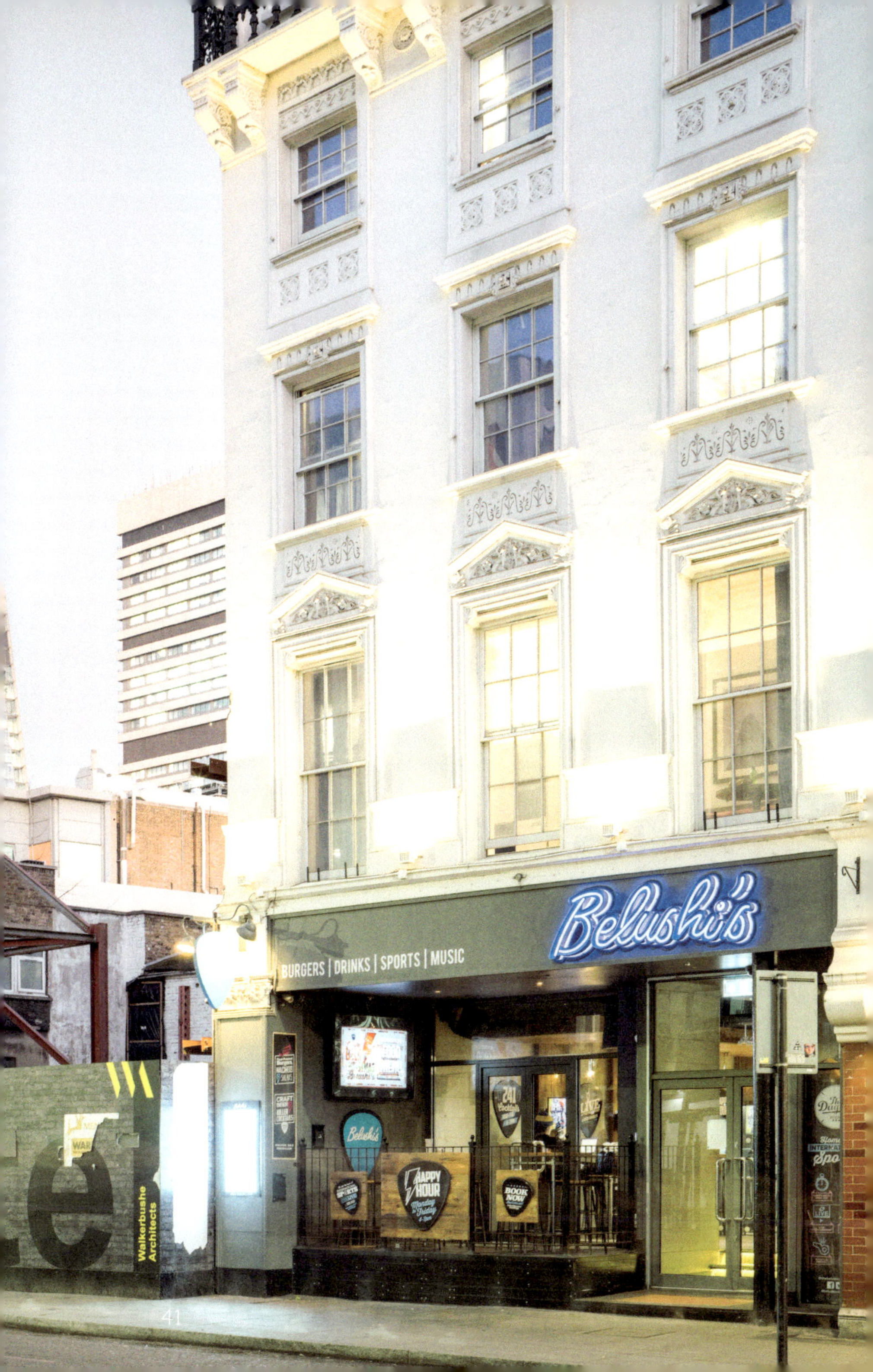
Belushi's
BURGERS | DRINKS | SPORTS | MUSIC
HAPPY HOUR
BOOK NOW
Walkerbushe Architects

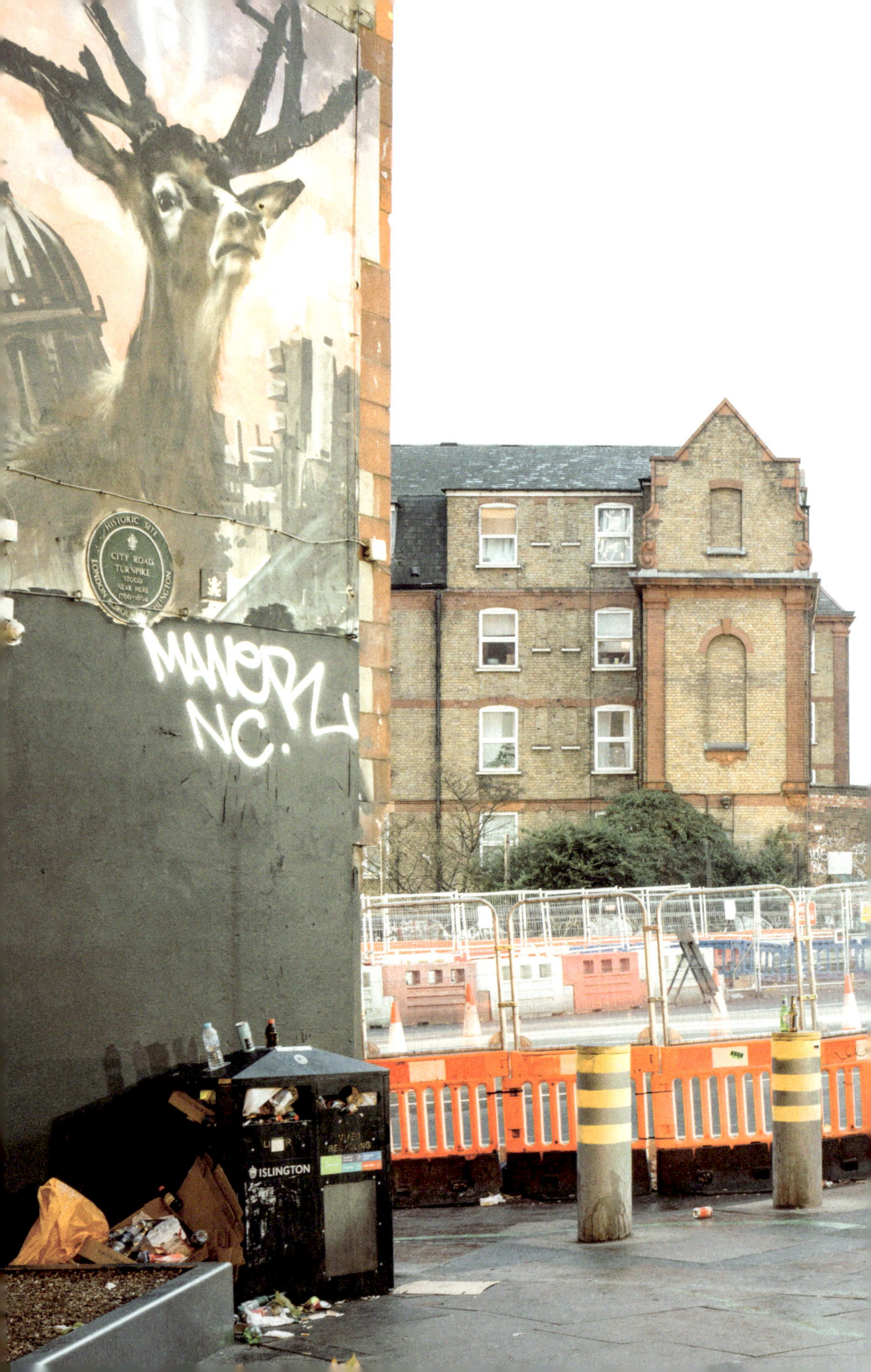
HISTORIC SITE
CITY ROAD TURNPIKE STOOD NEAR HERE 1760-1864
LONDON BOROUGH OF ISLINGTON
ISLINGTON
MIXED RECYCLING

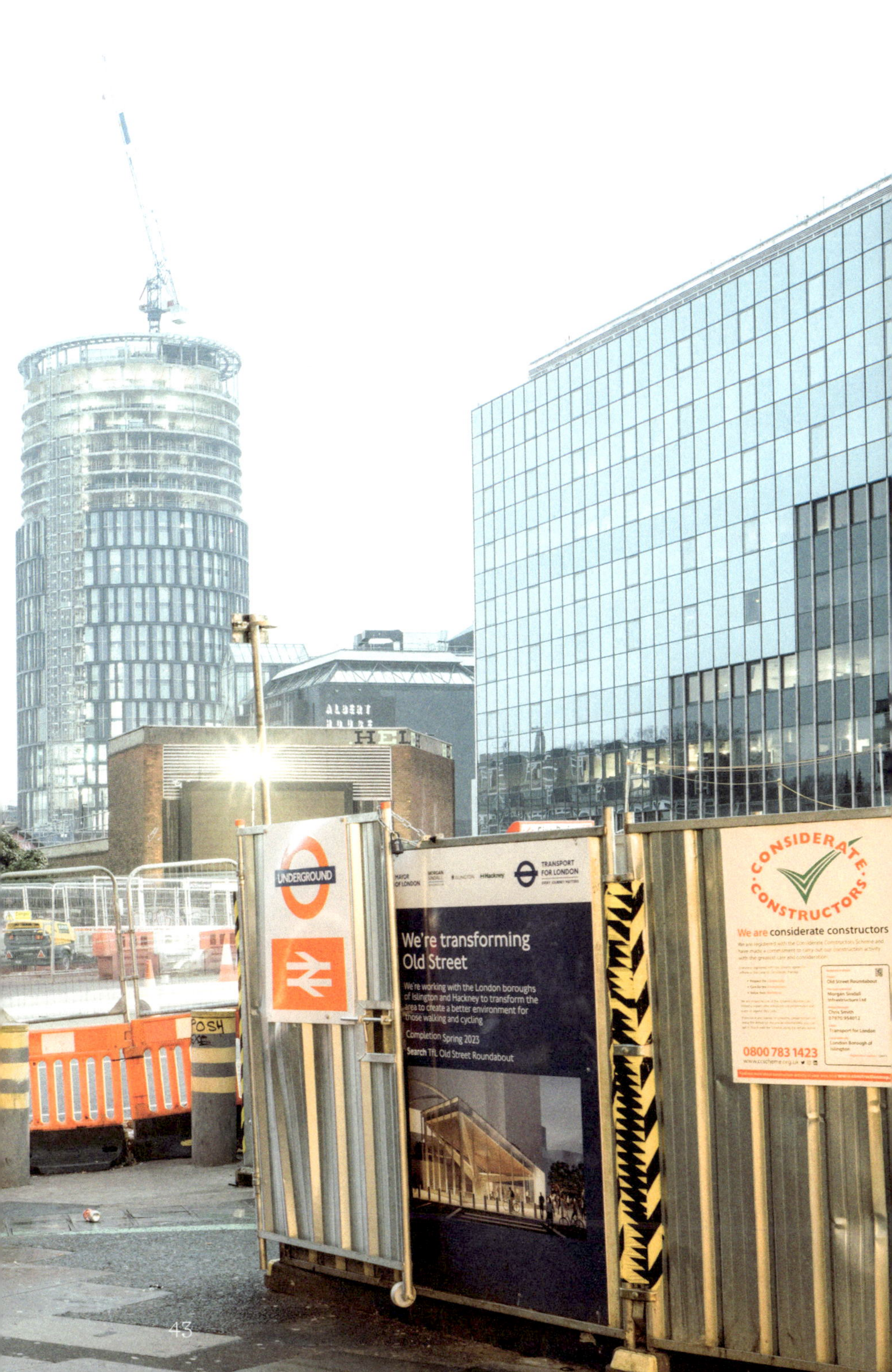
UNDERGROUND
TRANSPORT FOR LONDON
We're transforming Old Street
We're working with the London boroughs of Islington and Hackney to transform the area to create a better environment for those walking and cycling
Completion Spring 2023
Search TfL Old Street Roundabout
CONSIDERATE CONSTRUCTORS
We are considerate constructors
0800 783 1423
ALBERT
POSH

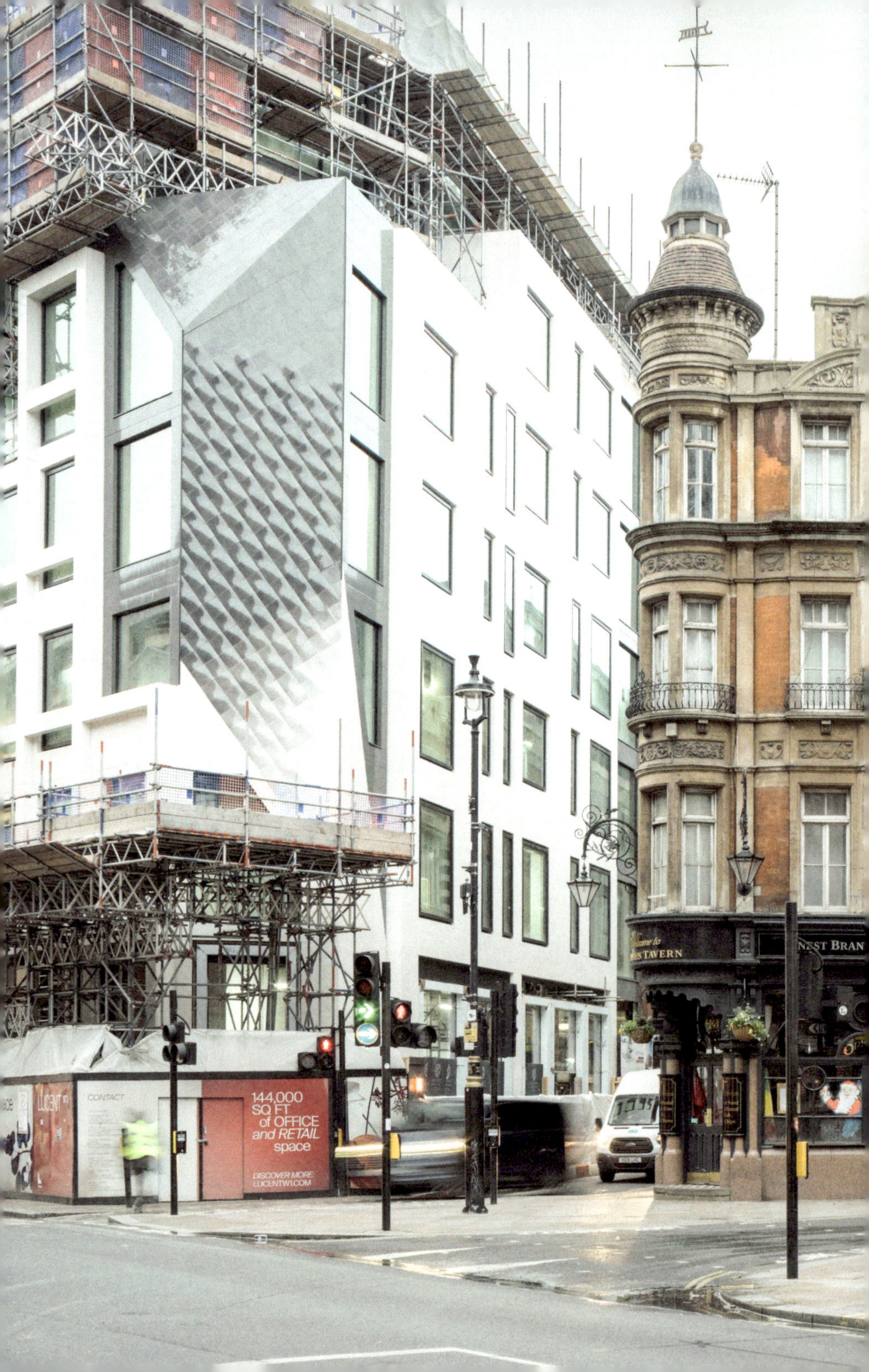
LUCENT
CONTACT
144,000
SQ FT
of OFFICE
and RETAIL
space
DISCOVER MORE:
LUCENTW1.COM
NEST BRAN

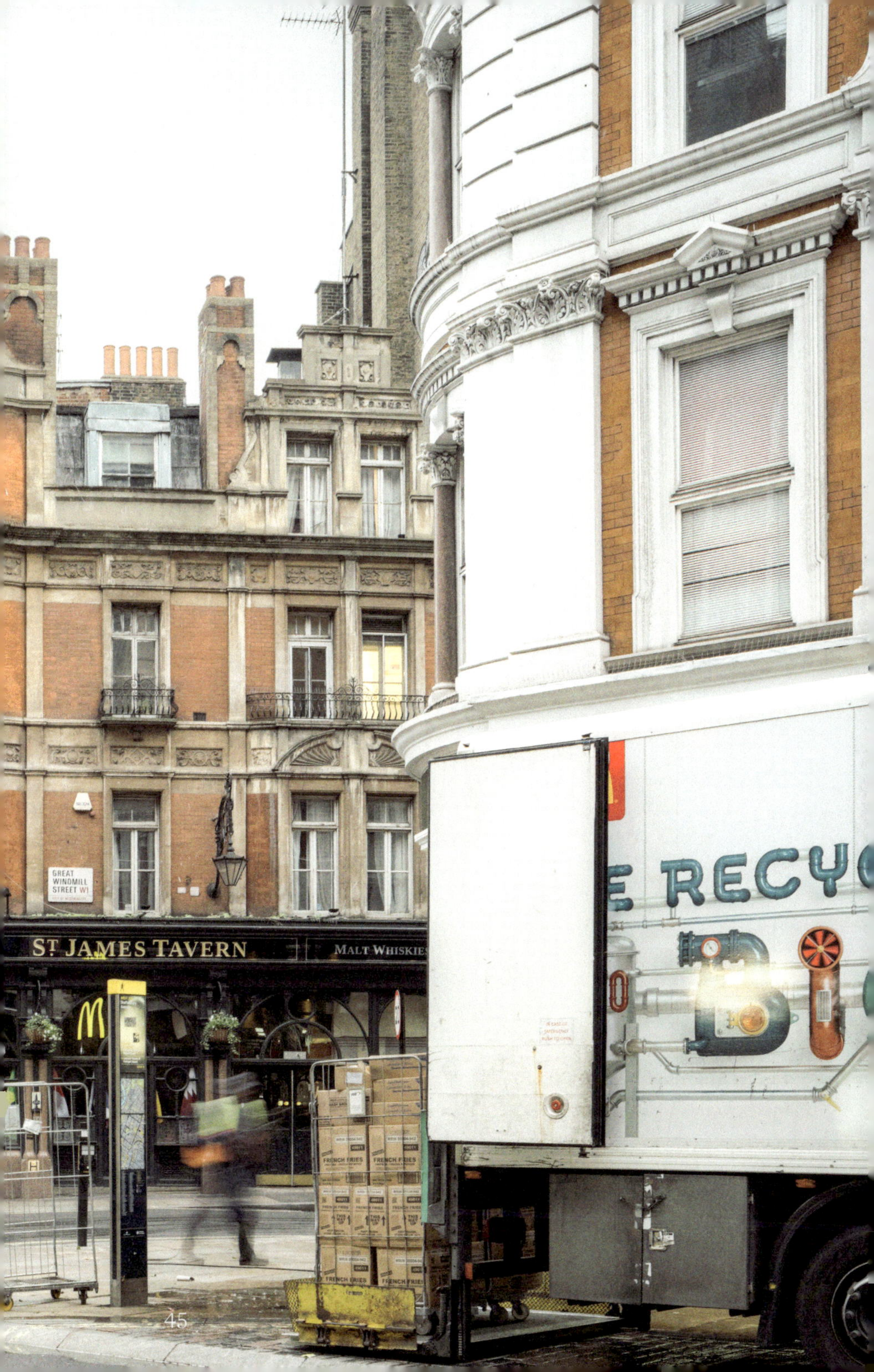
GREAT
WINDMILL
STREET W1
ST JAMES TAVERN
MALT WHISKIES
E RECYC
FRENCH FRIES

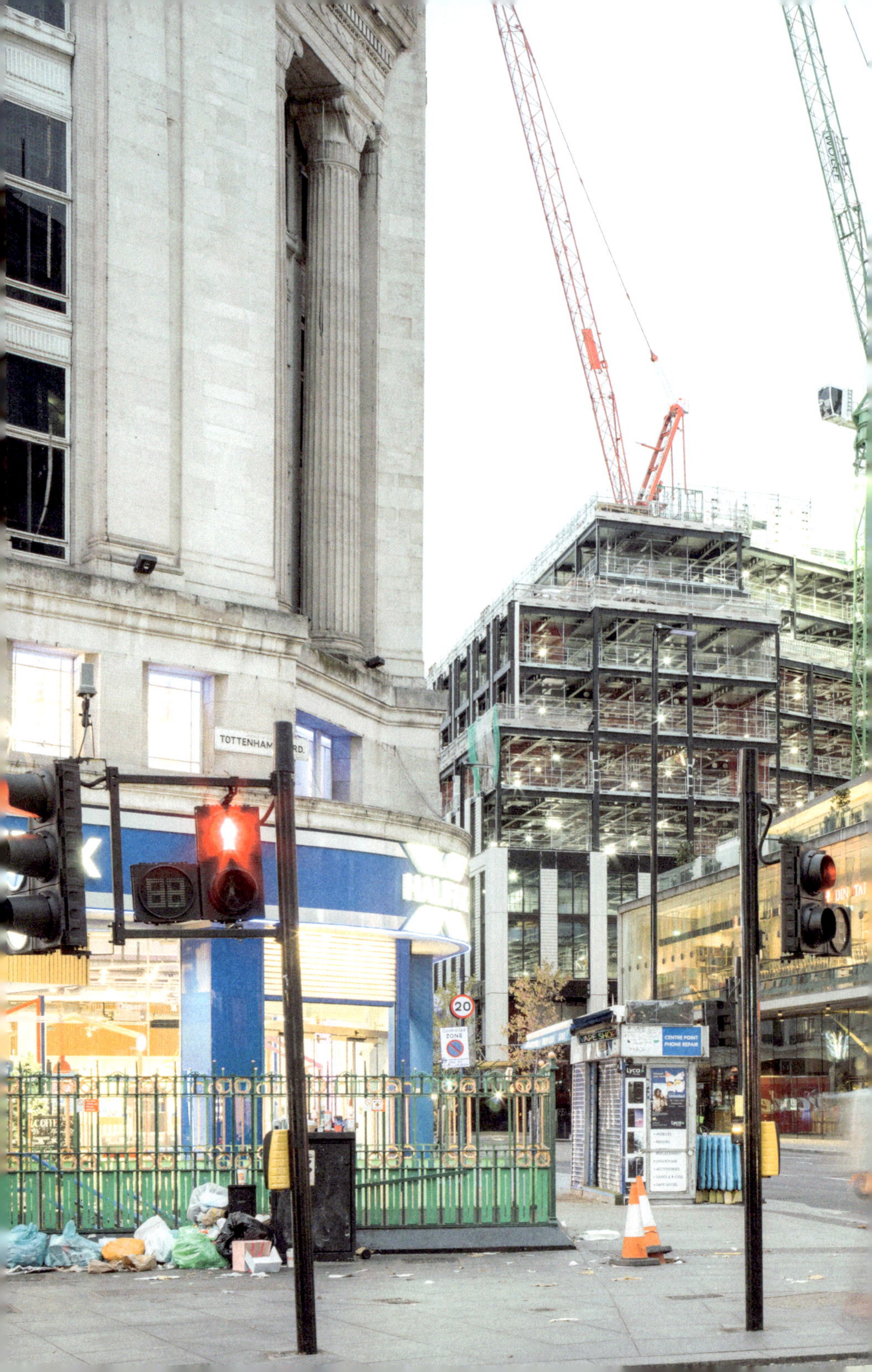
TOTTENHAM
RD.
20
VAPE SHOP
CENTRE POINT
PHONE REPAIR

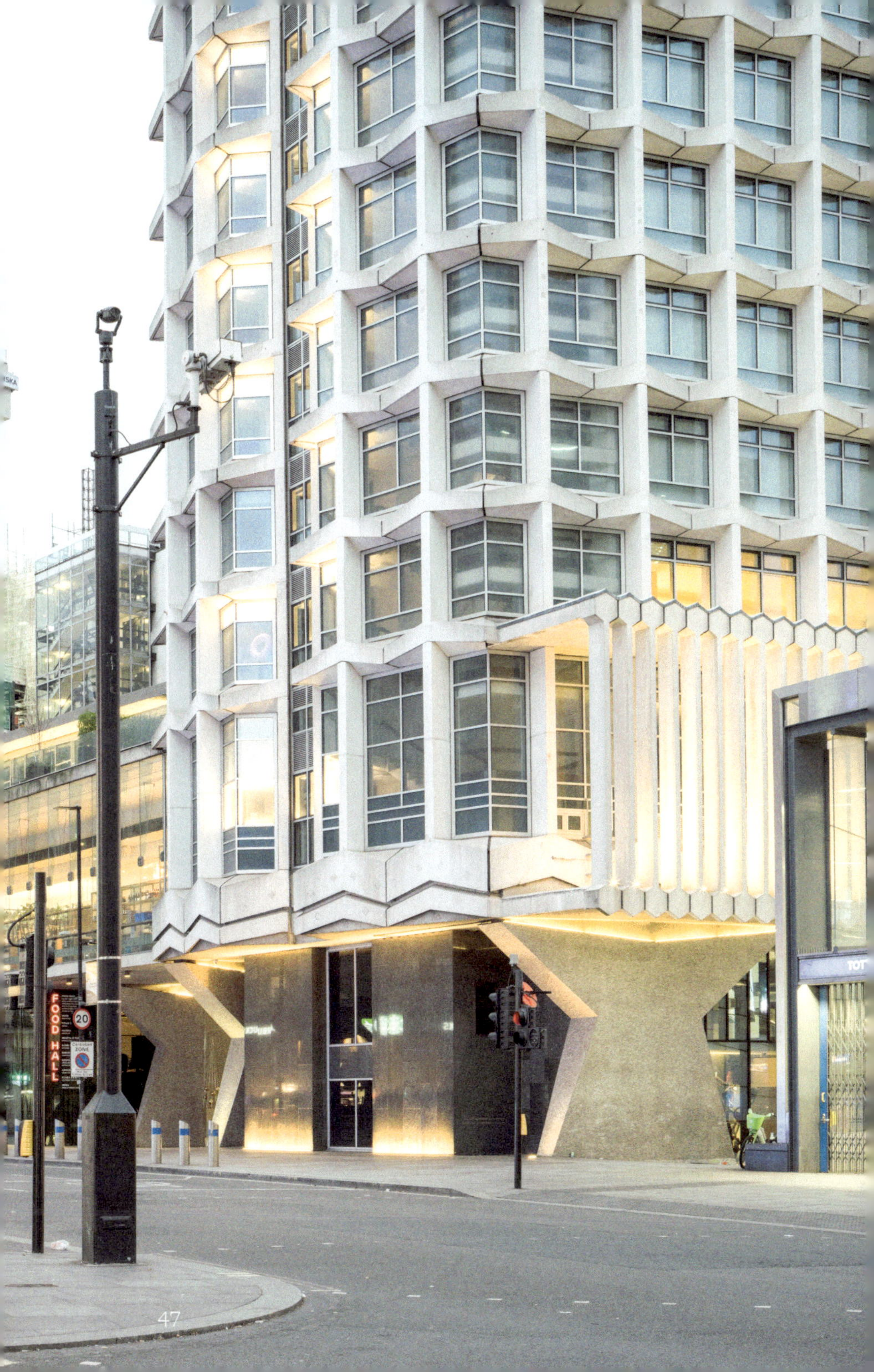
FOOD HALL
20

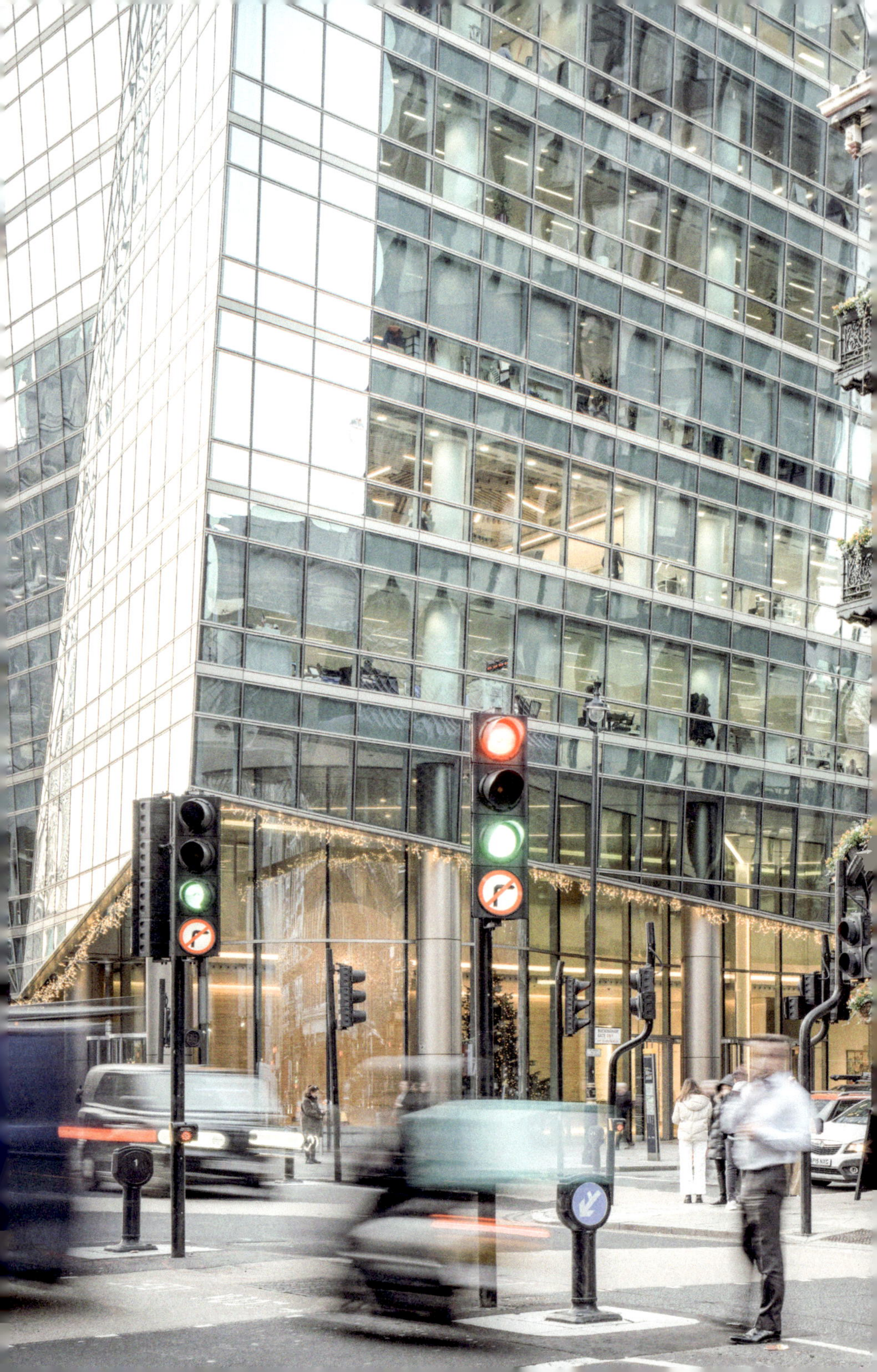

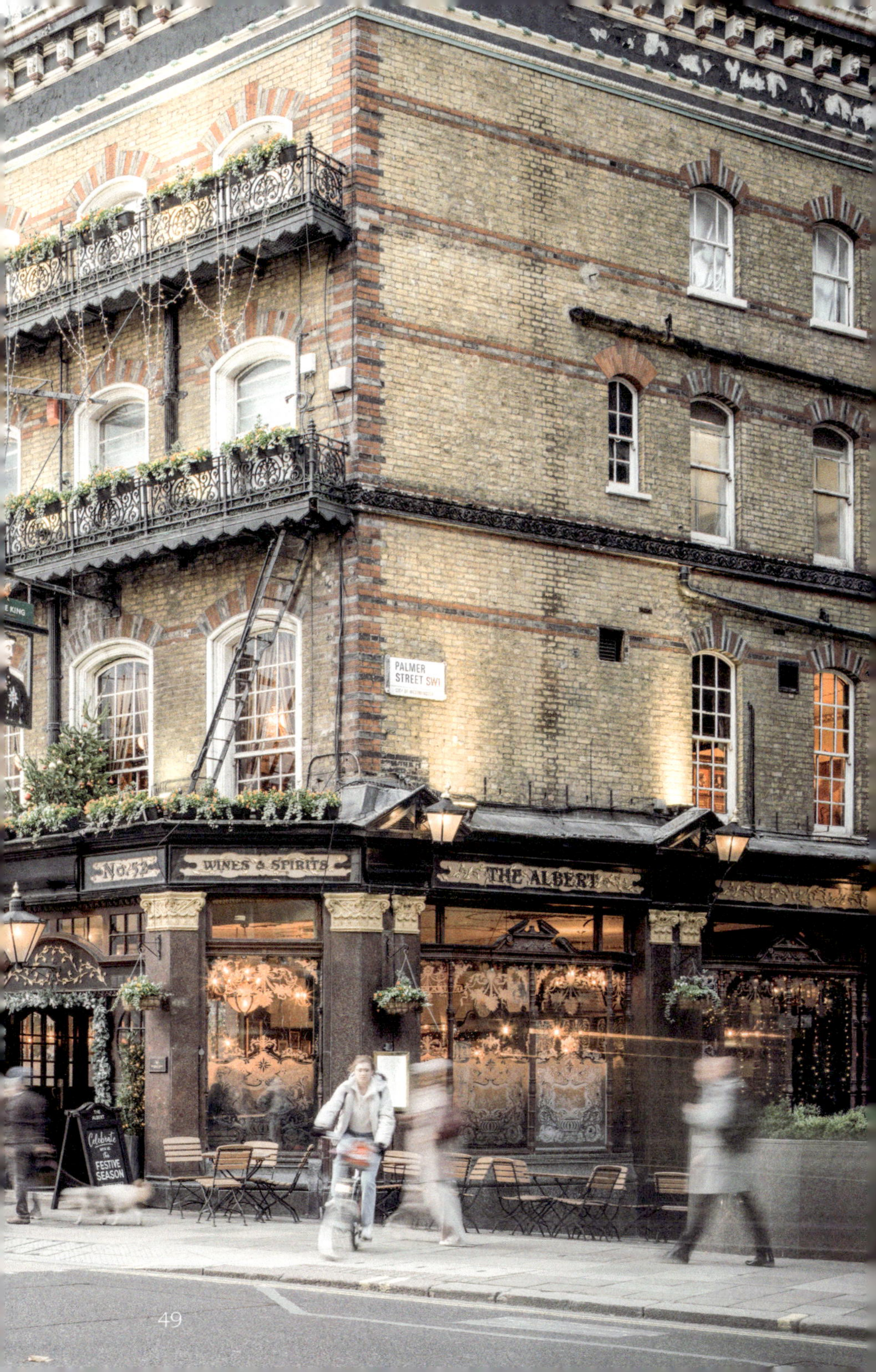
PALMER
STREET SW1
No 52
WINES & SPIRITS
THE ALBERT
Celebrate
FESTIVE
SEASON

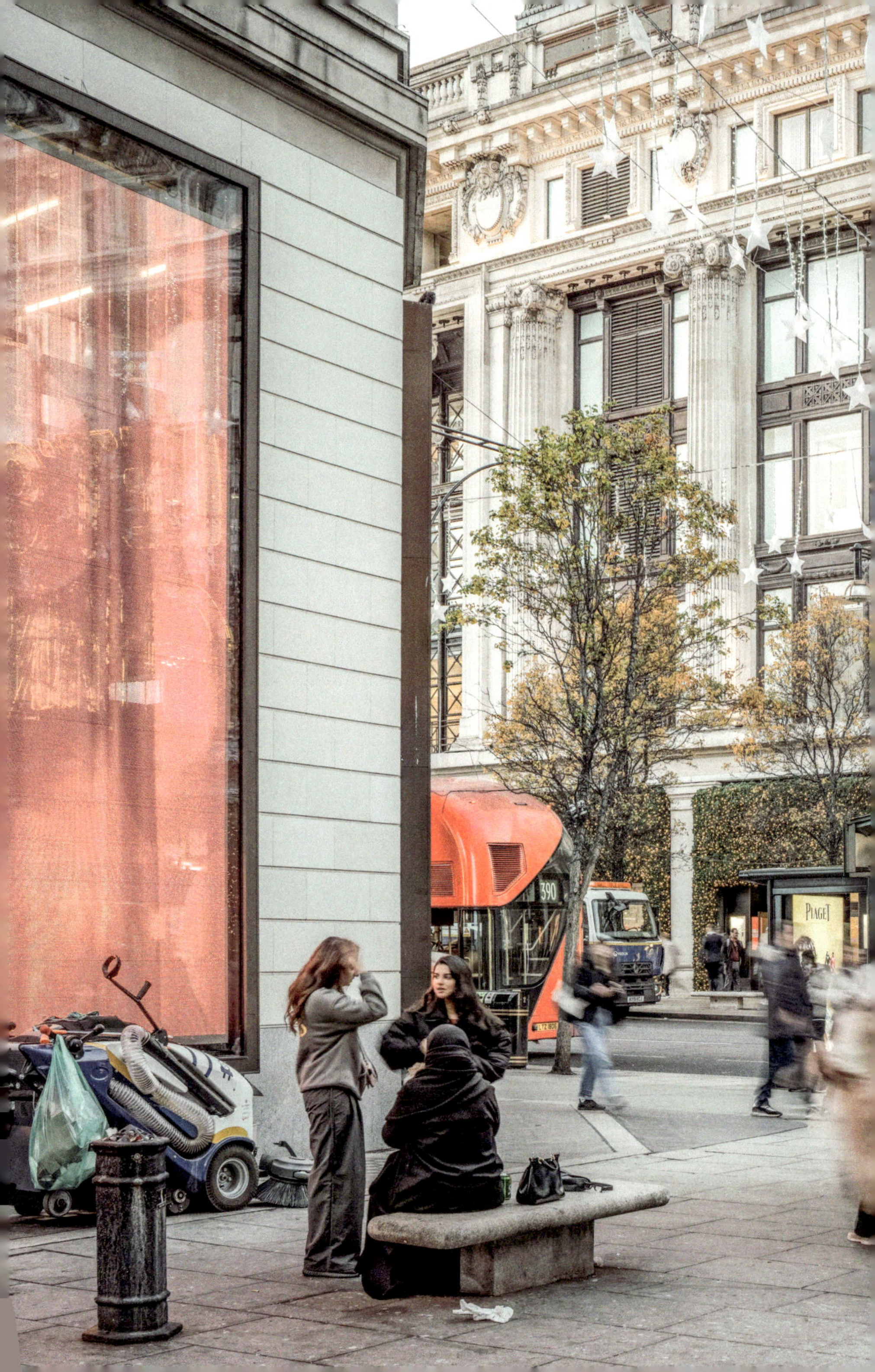
390
PIAGET

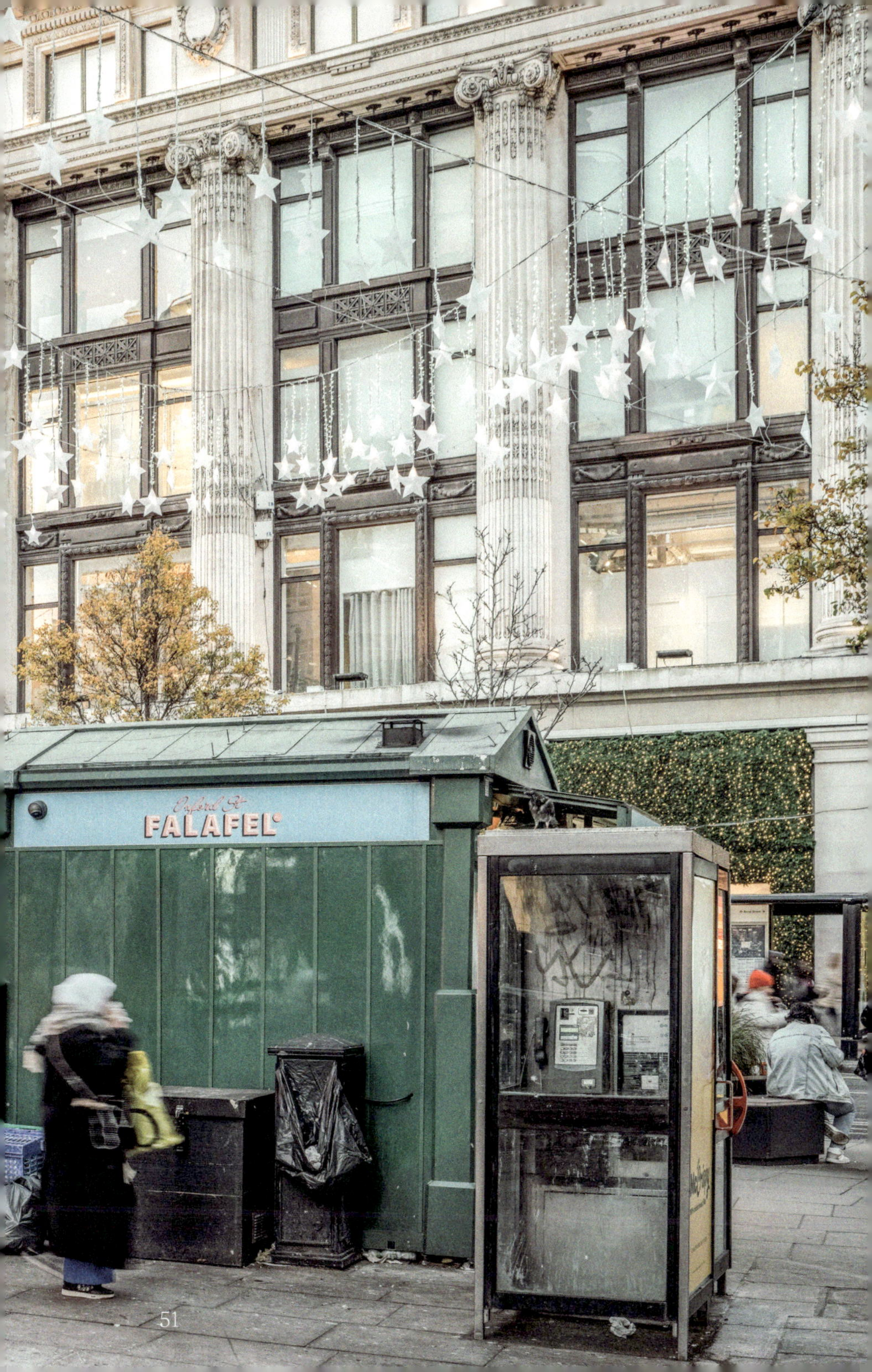
Oxford St
FALAFEL

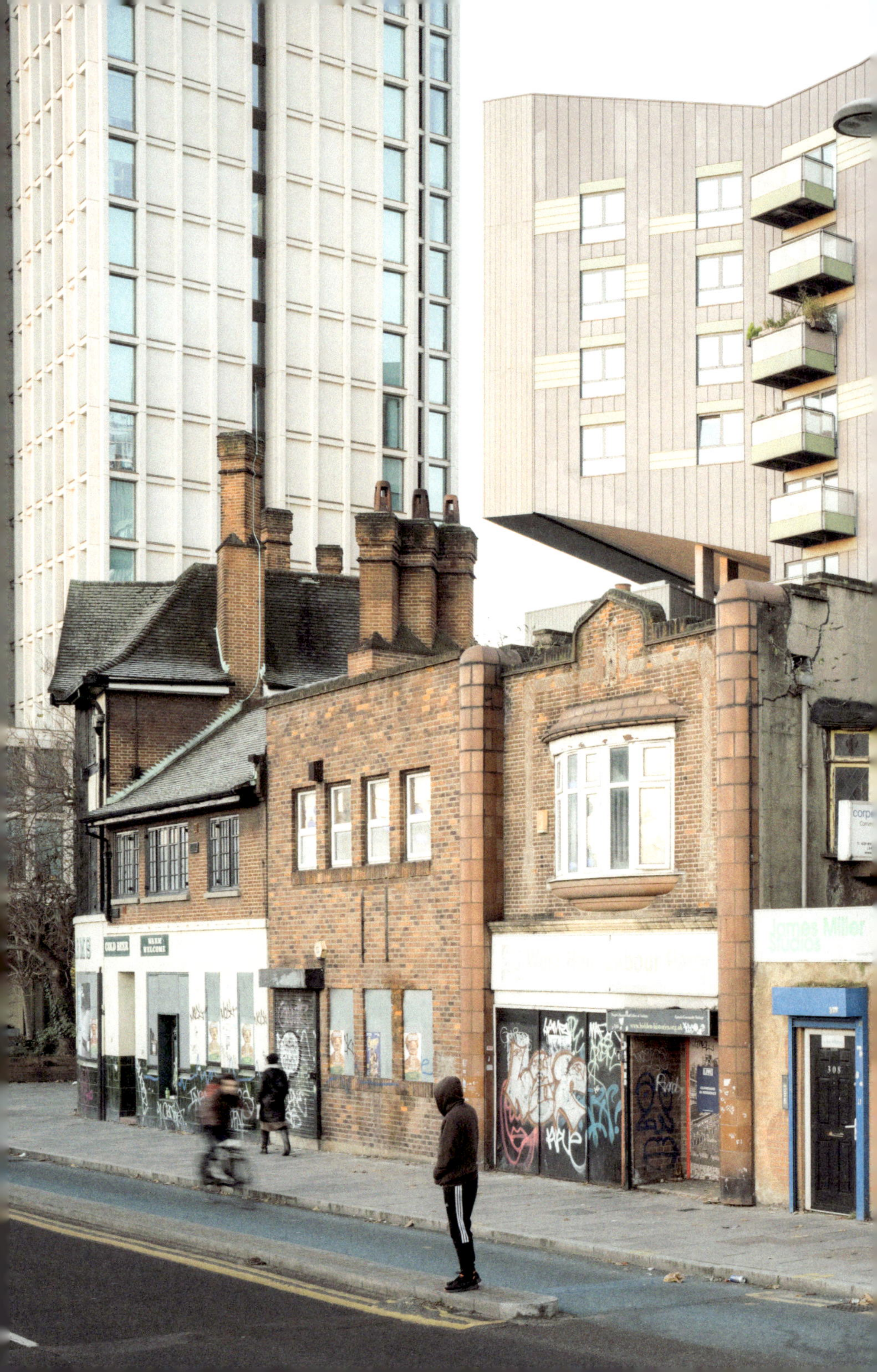
COLD BEER
WARM WELCOME
James Miller
Studios
308

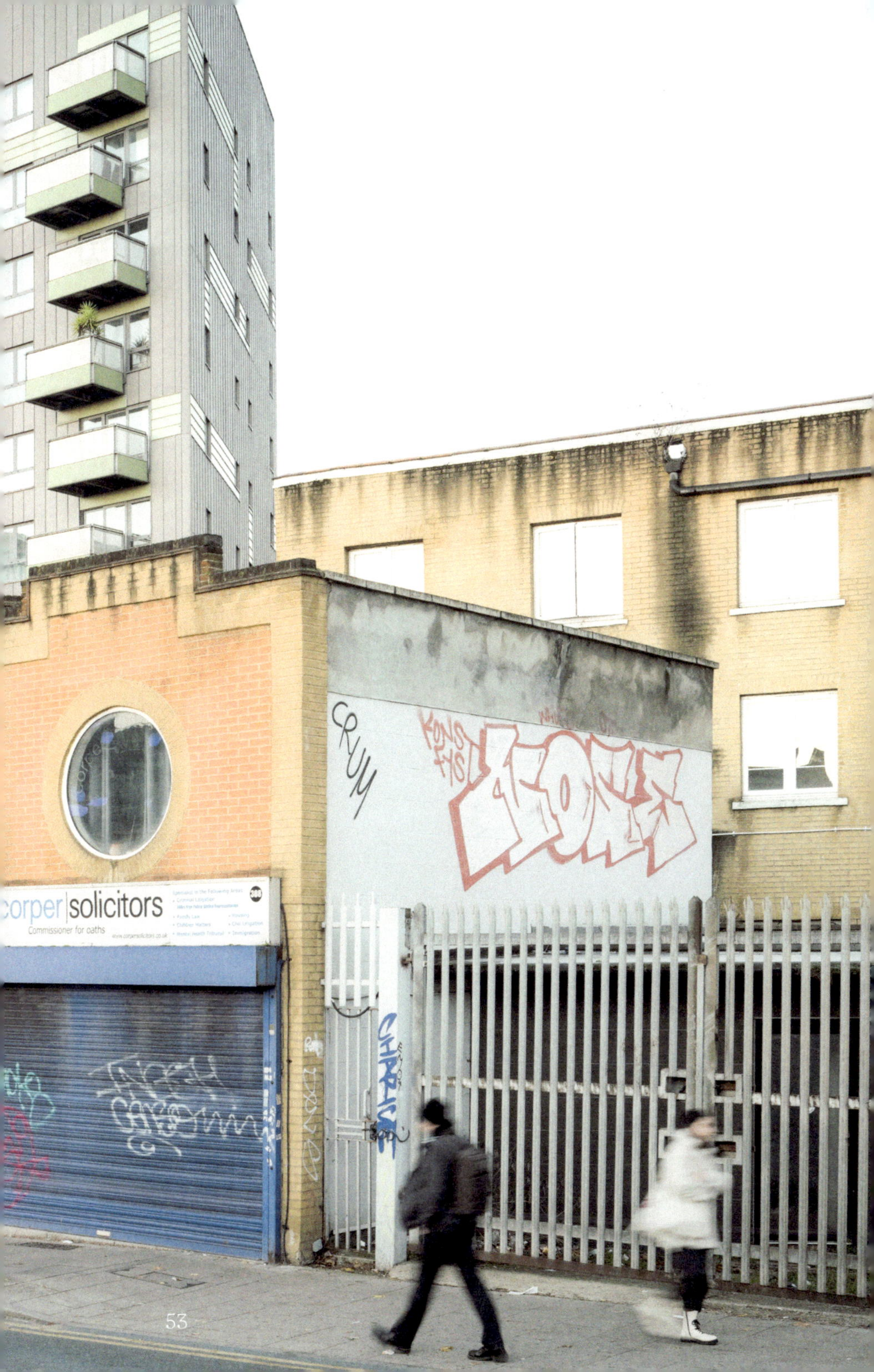
corper|solicitors
Commissioner for oaths

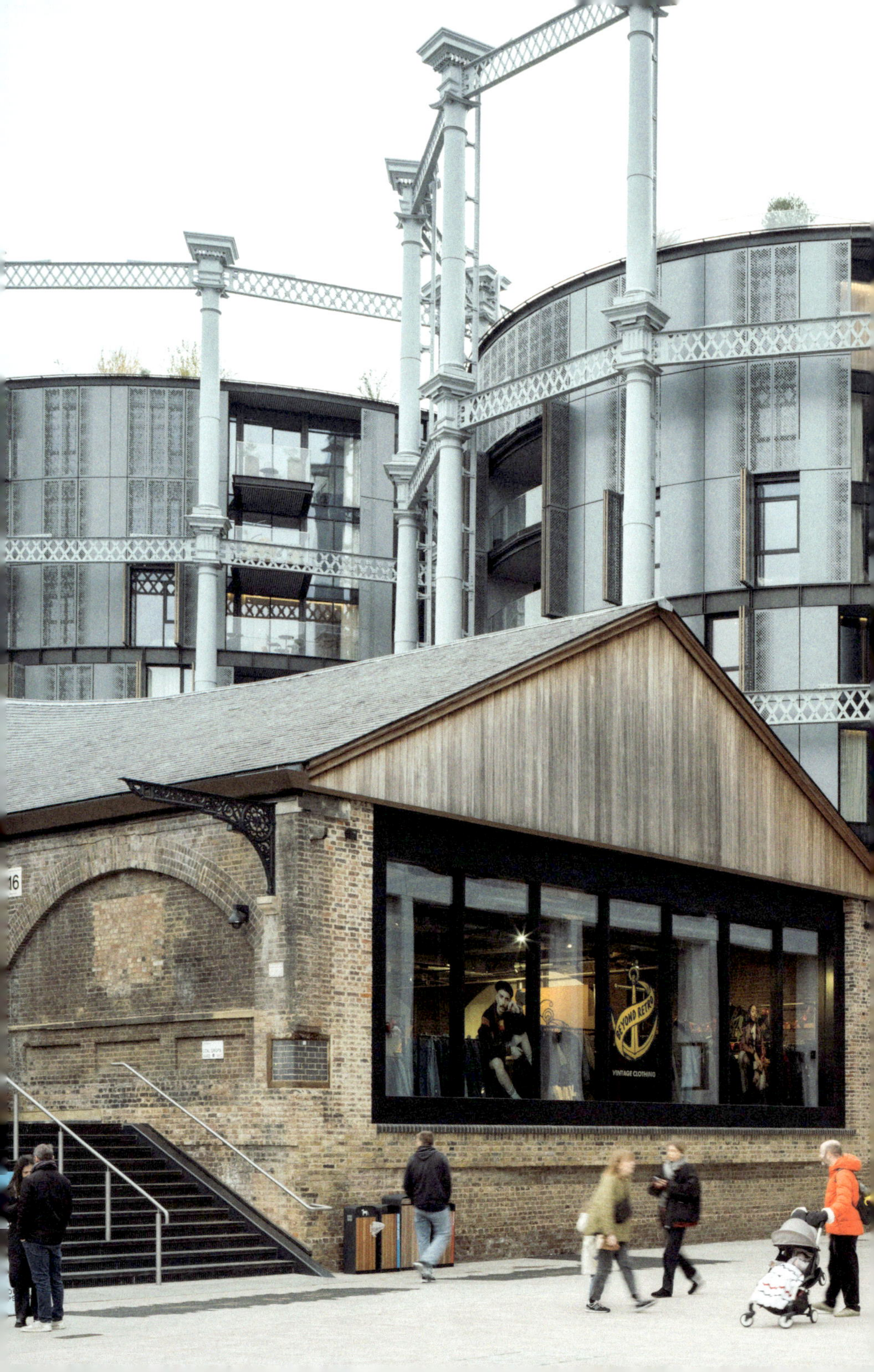
16
BEYOND RETRO
VINTAGE CLOTHING

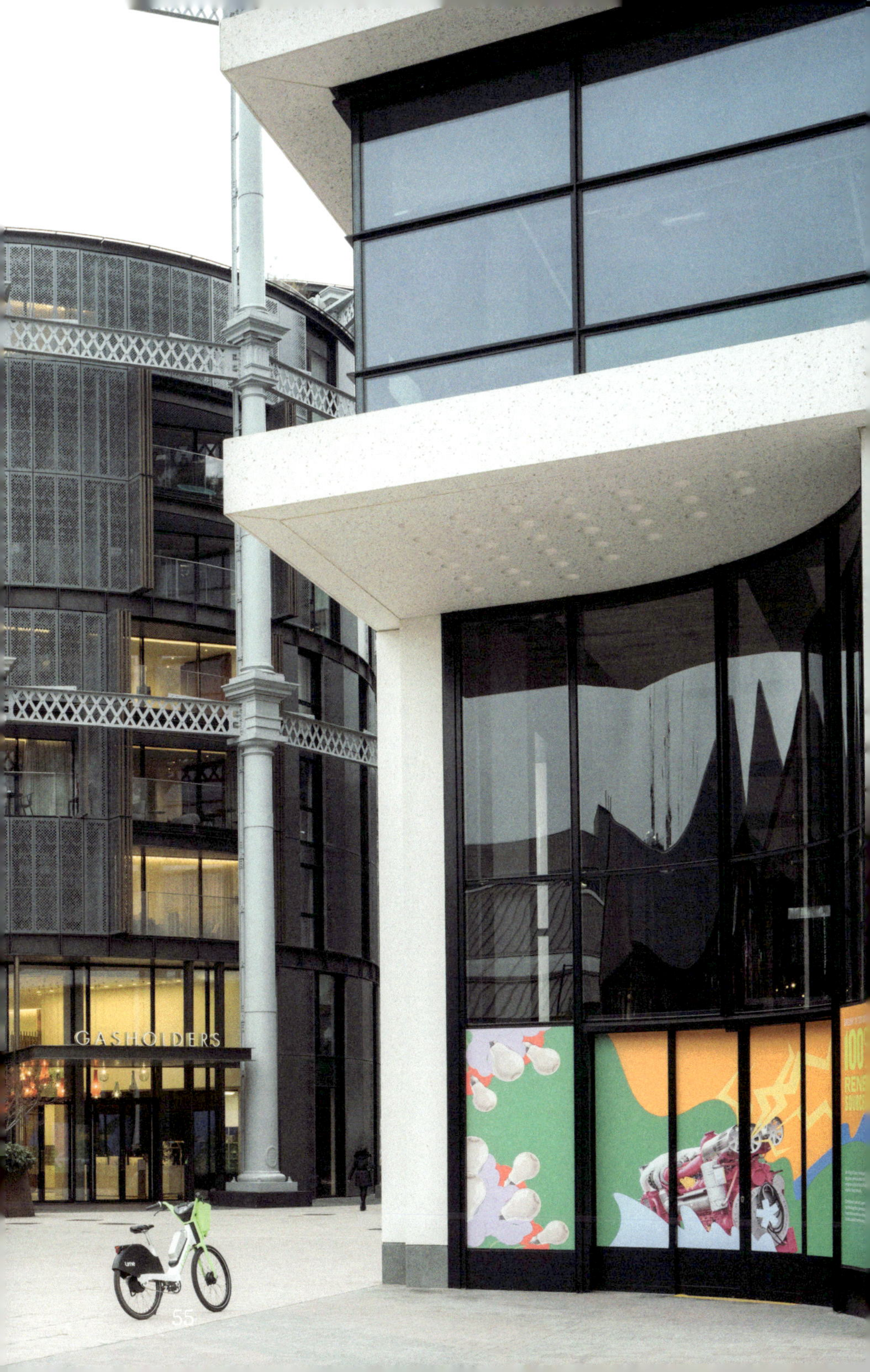
GASHOLDERS

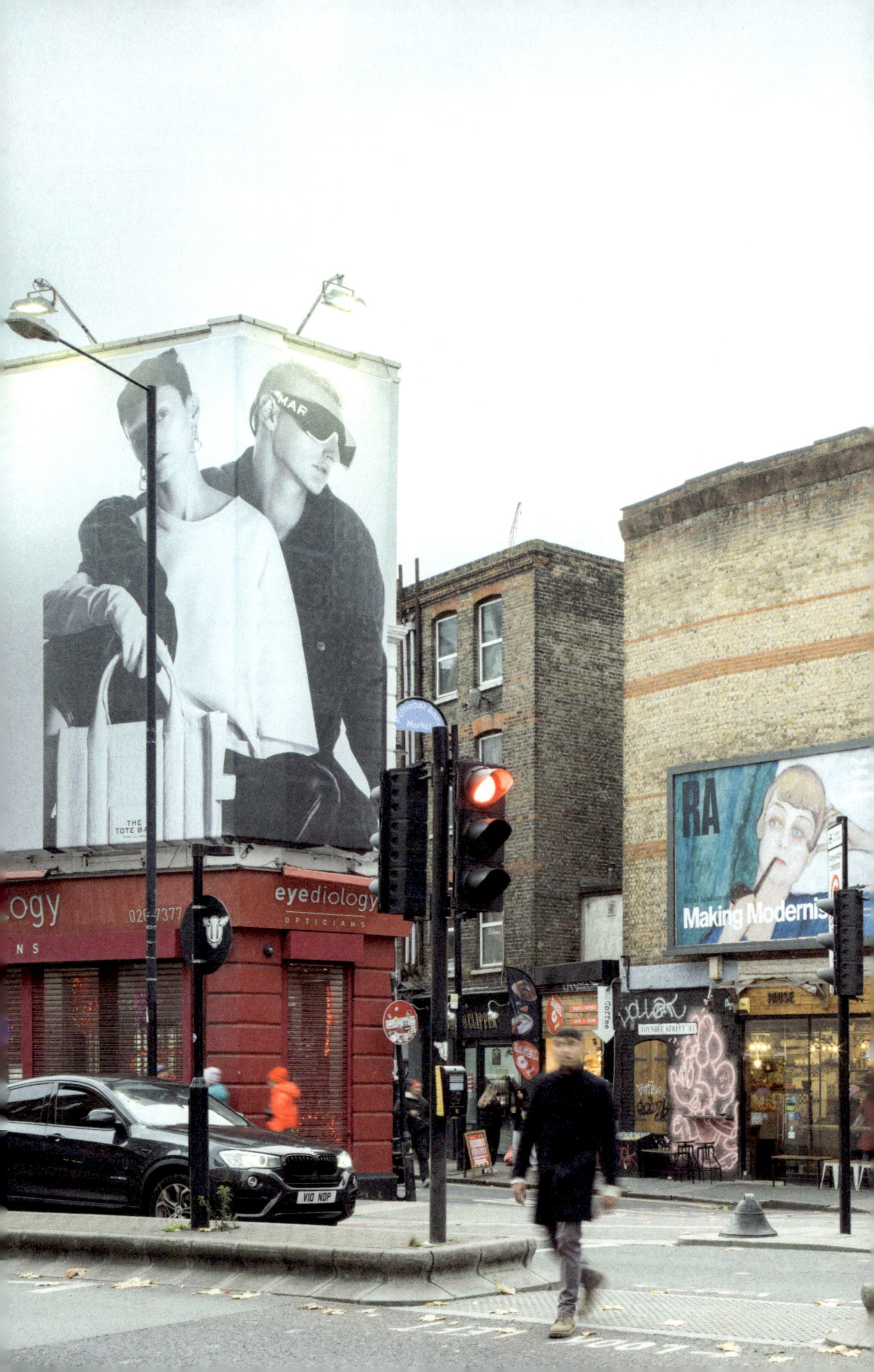
eyediology
OPTICIANS
RA
Making
Coffee
TOYNBEE STREET E1
V10 NDP

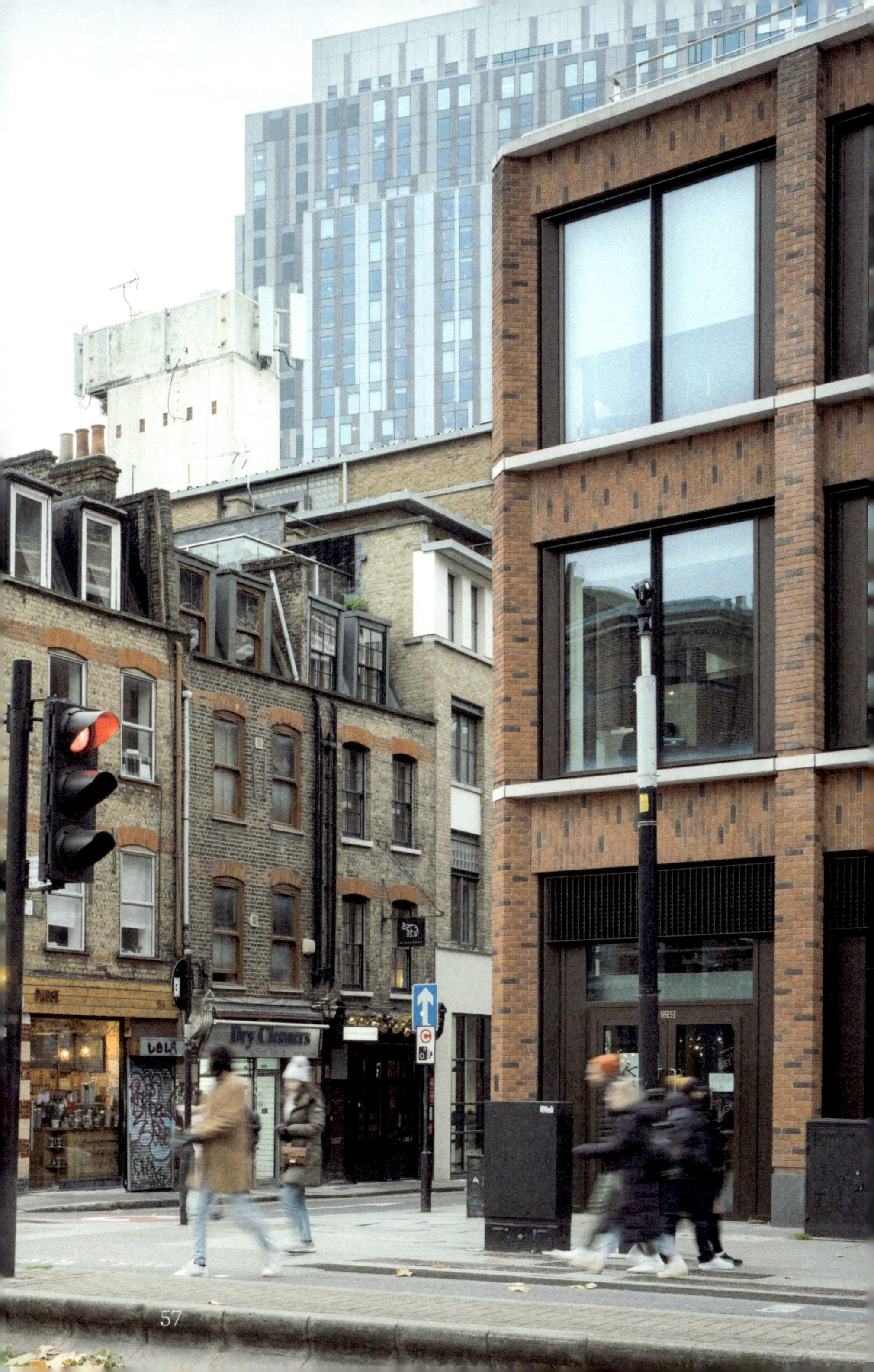
Dry Cleaners

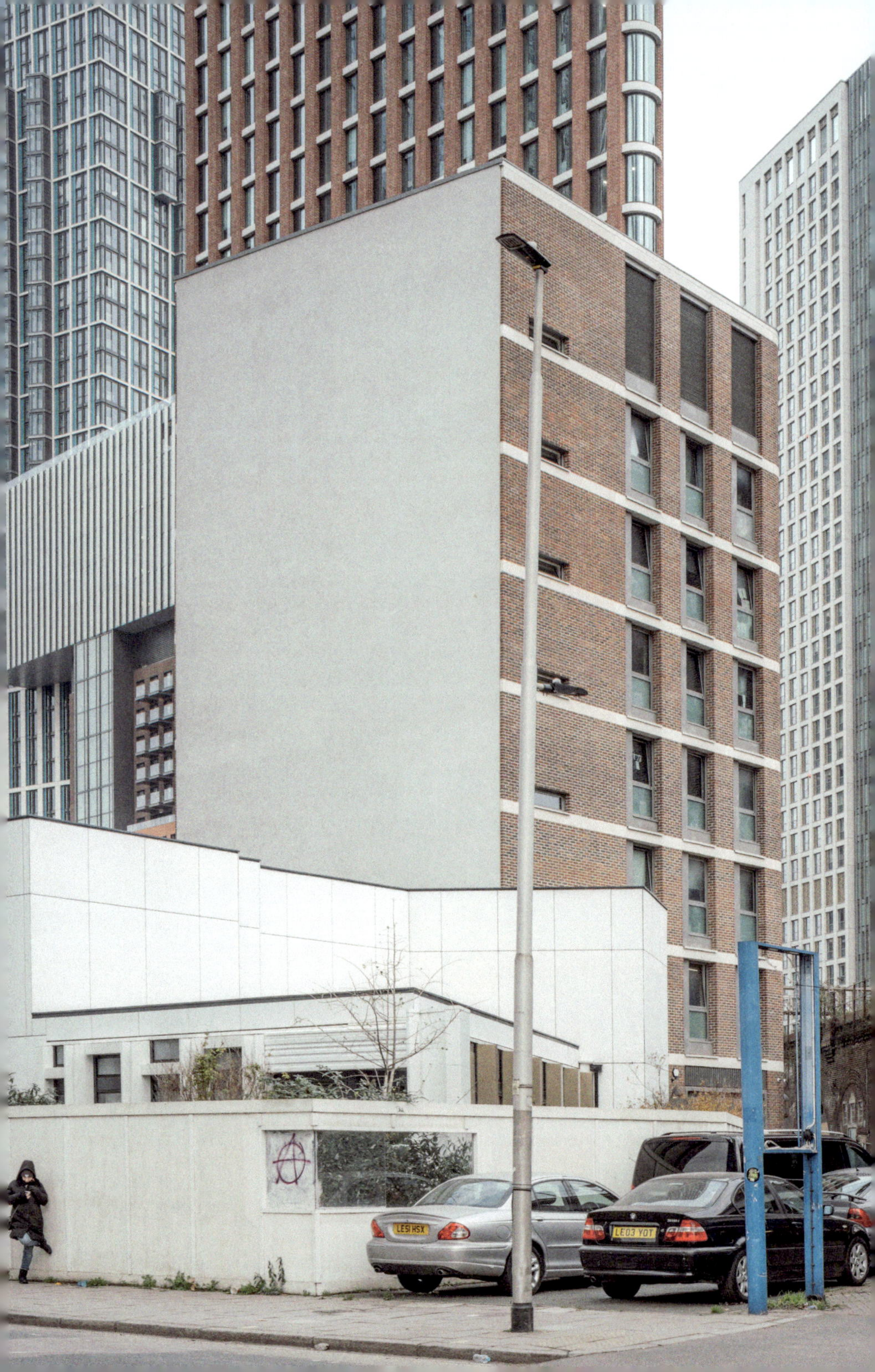
LE51 HSX
LE03 YOT

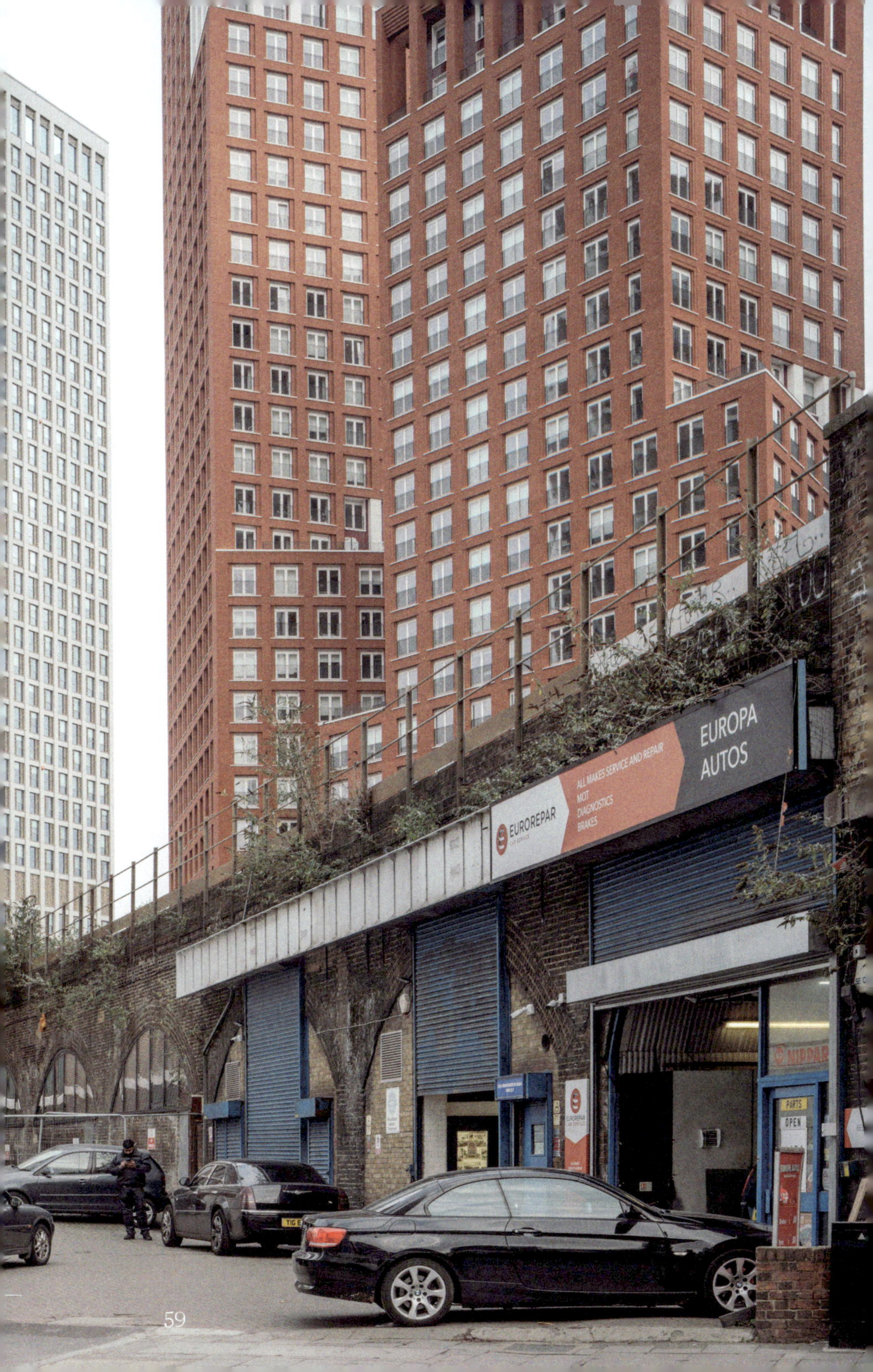
EUROPA
AUTOS
EUROREPAR
ALL MAKES SERVICE AND REPAIR
MOT
DIAGNOSTICS
BRAKES
PARTS
OPEN

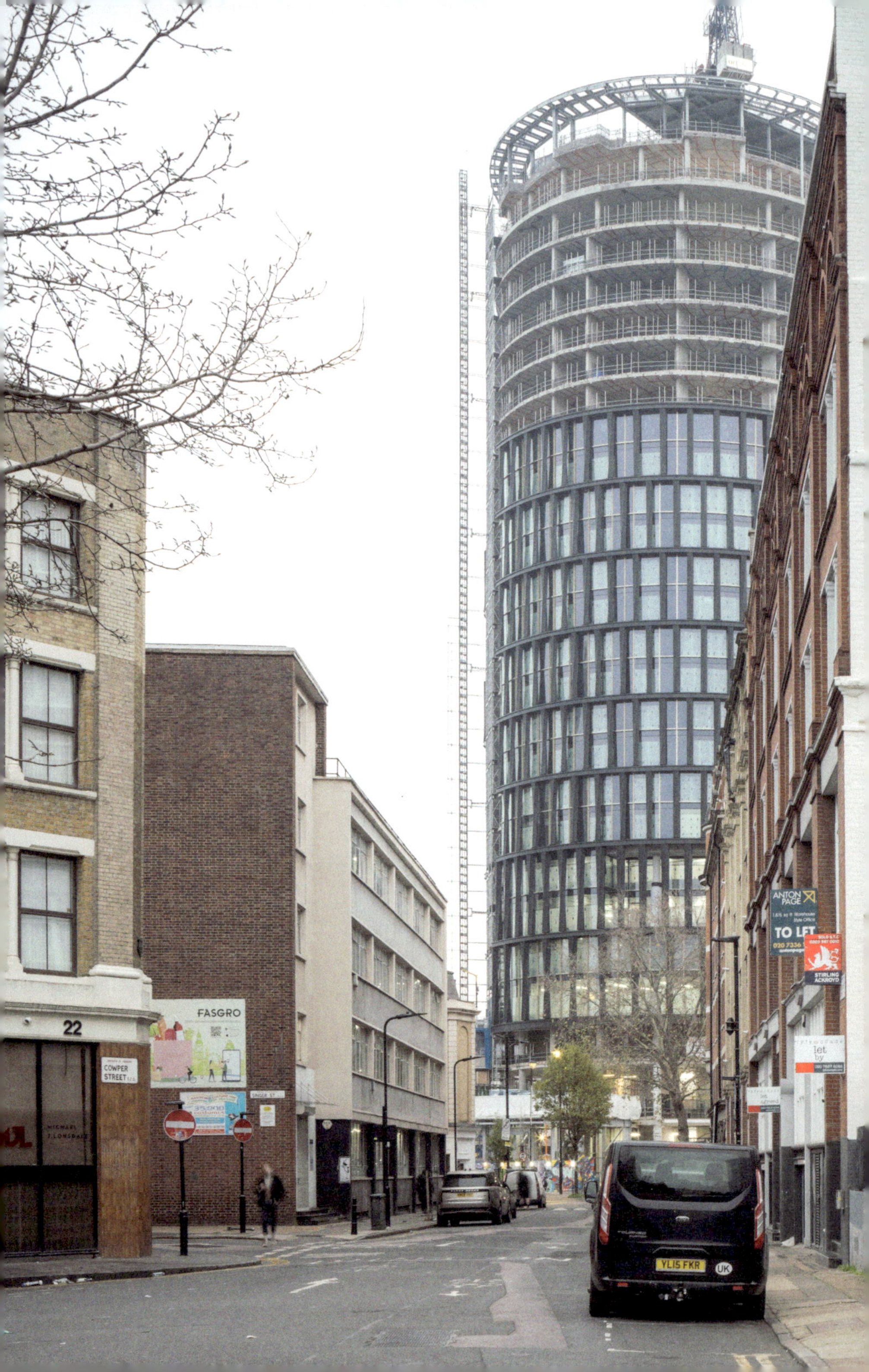
22
COWPER
STREET
FASGRO
ANTON
PAGE
TO LET
STIRLING
ACKROYD
YL15 FKR
UK

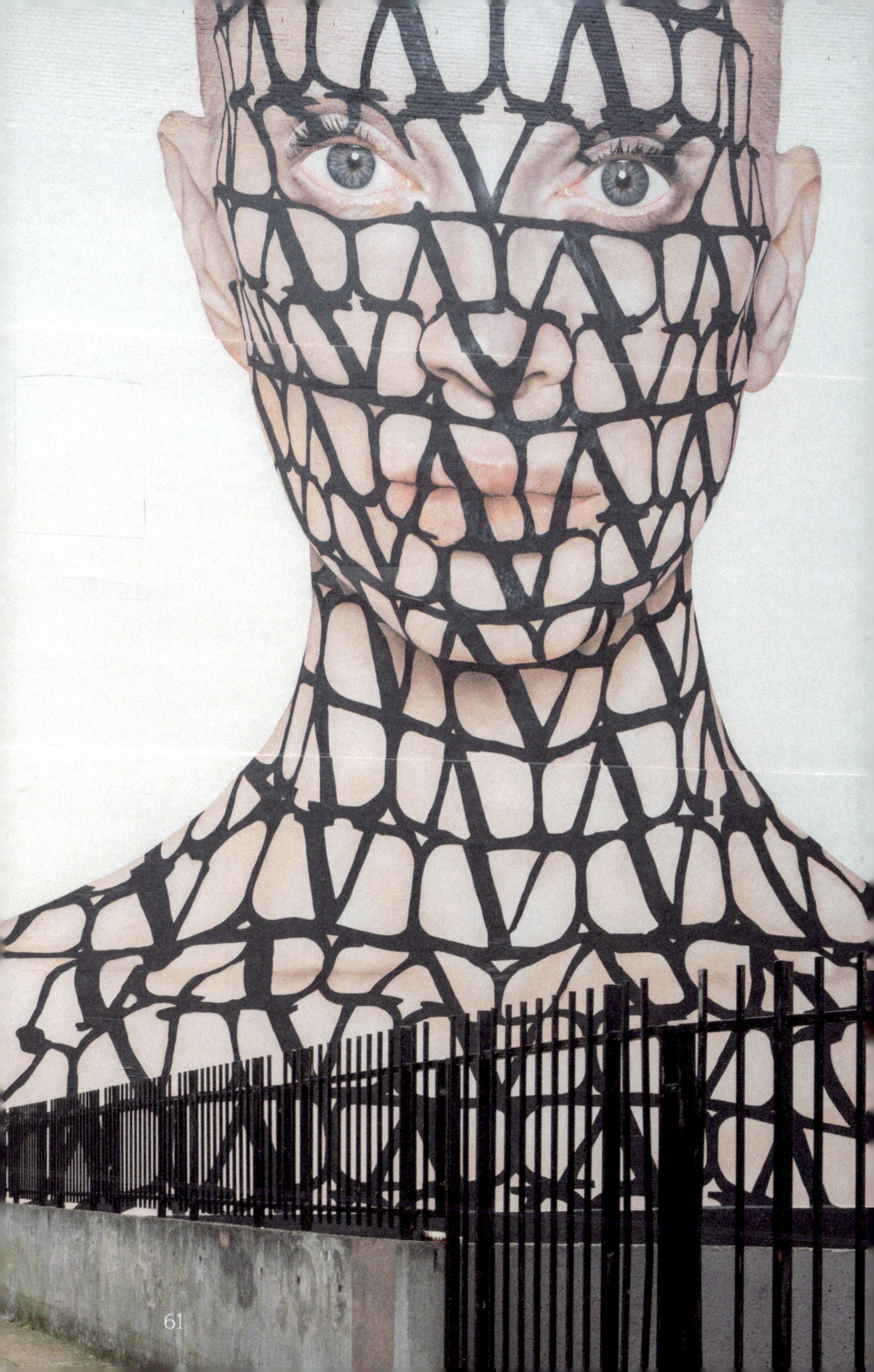

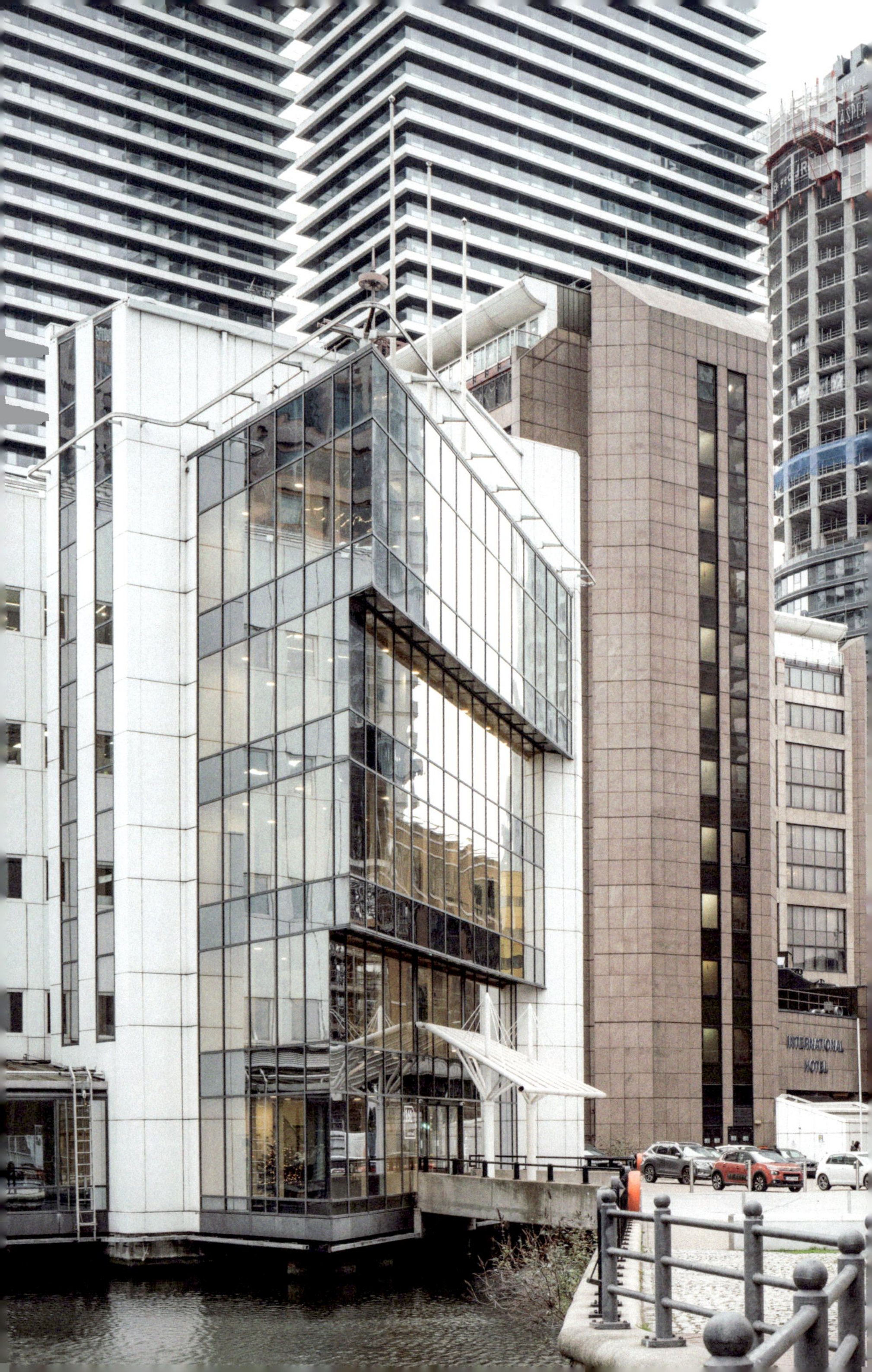
INTERNATIONAL
HOTEL

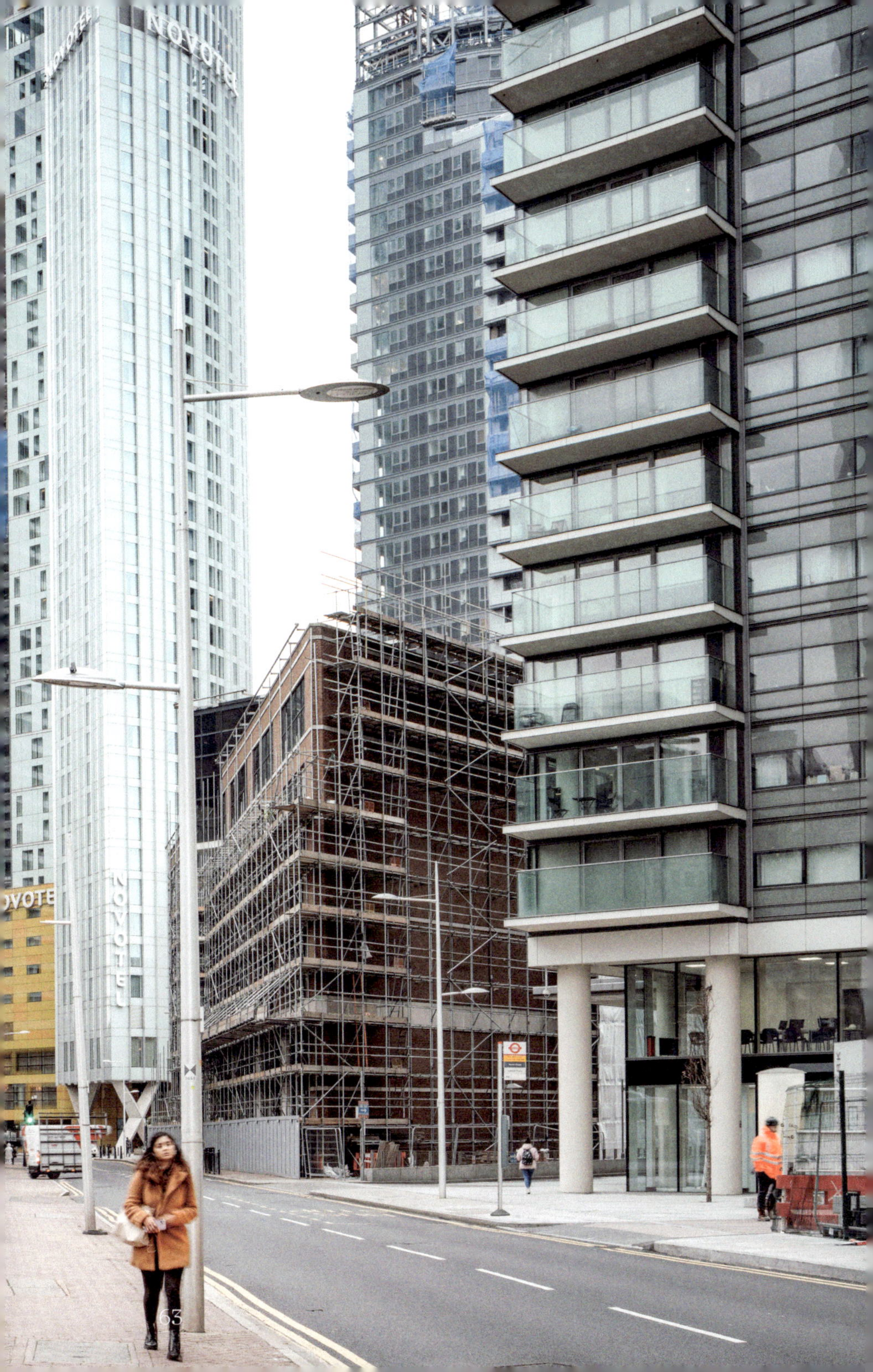
NOVOTEL
NOVOTEL

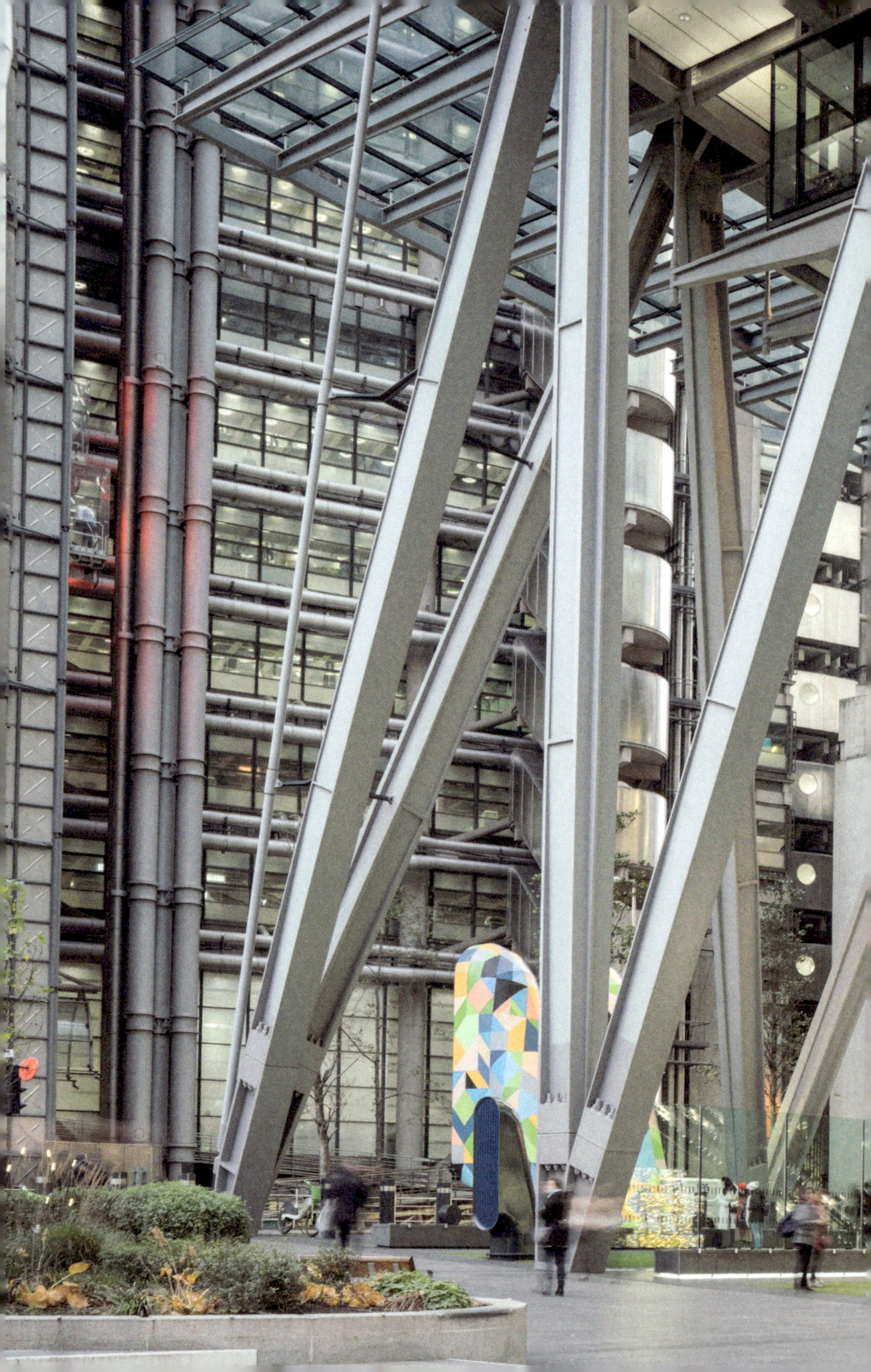

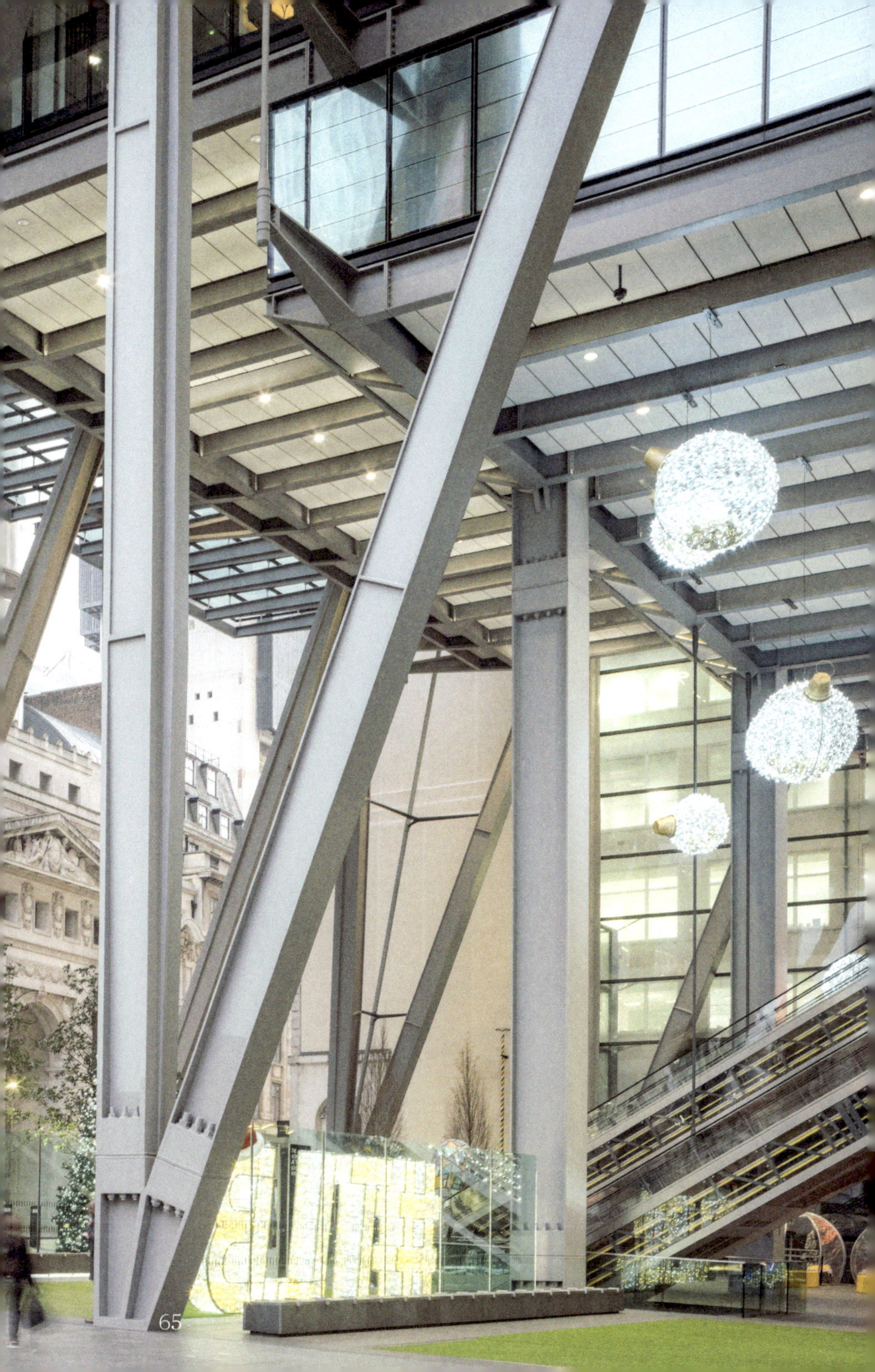

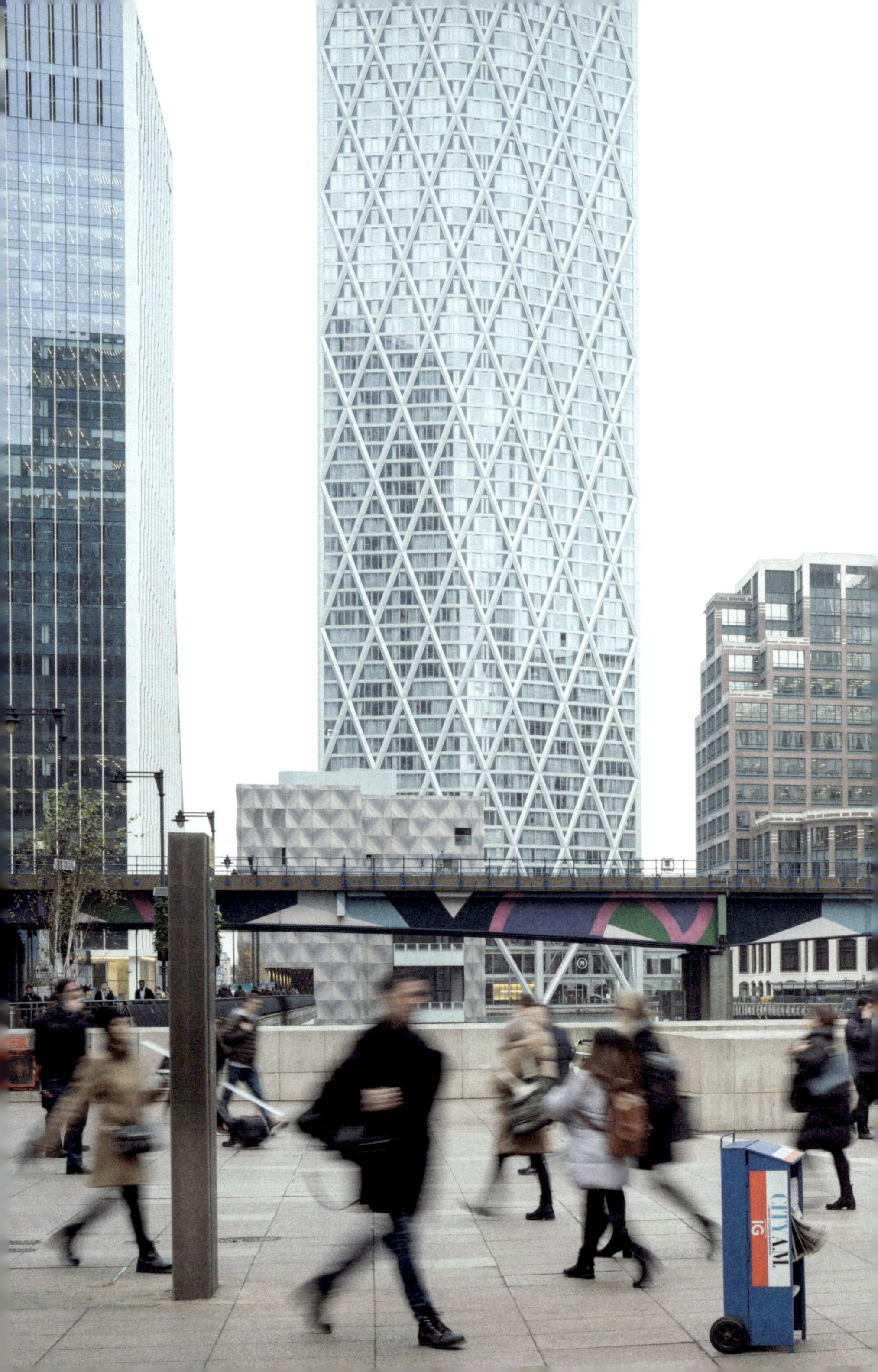
CITY A.M.
IG

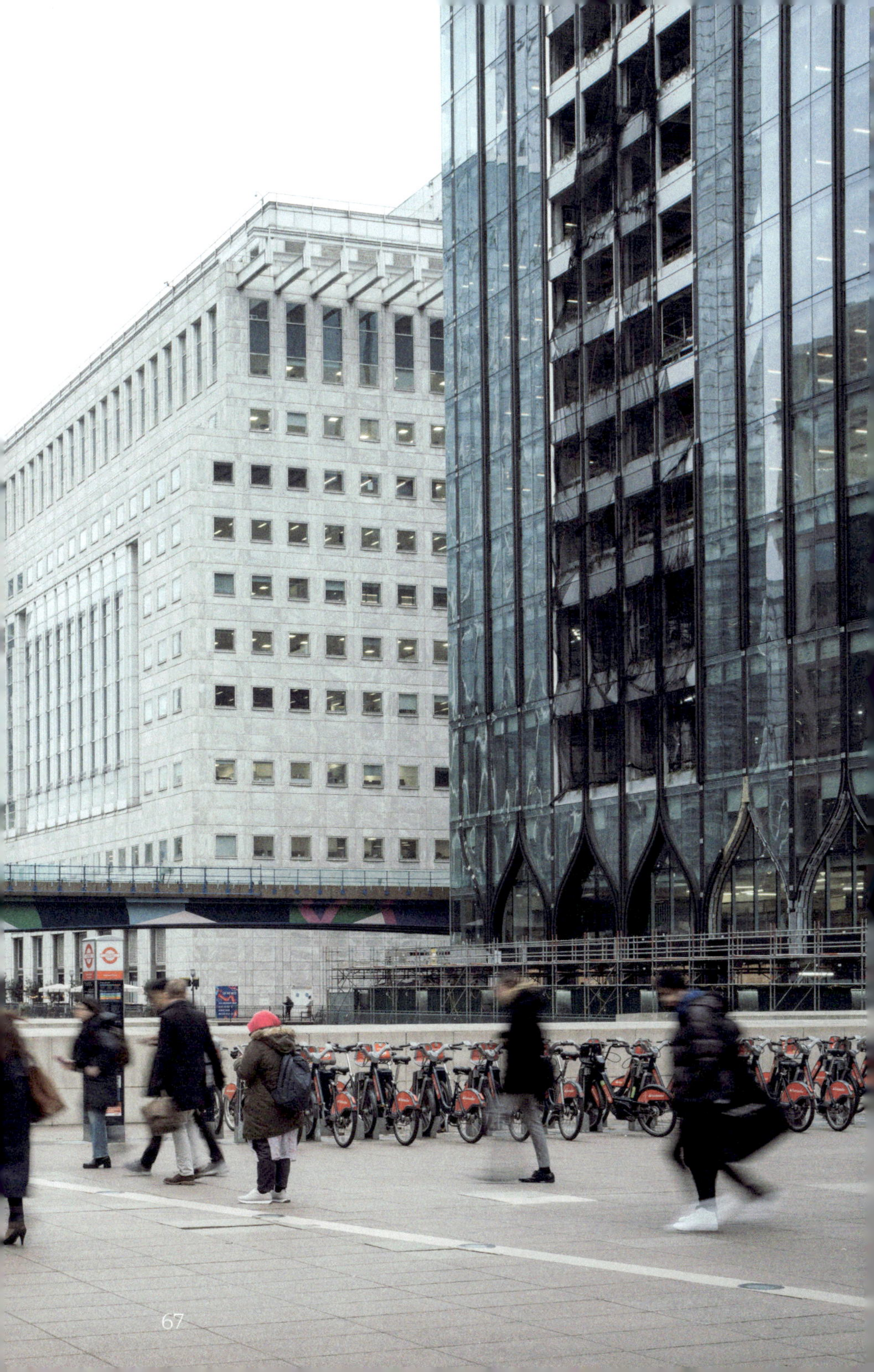

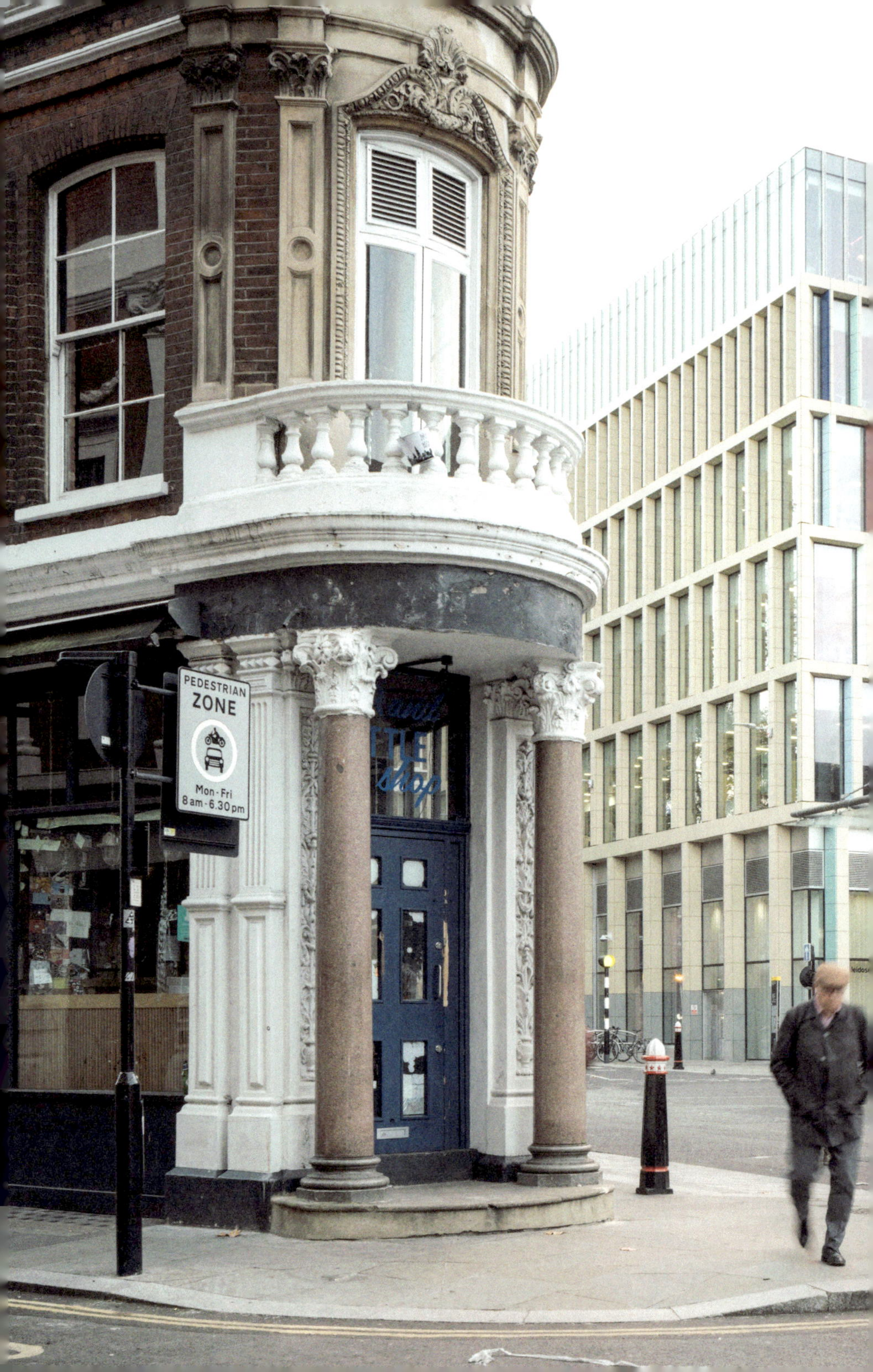
PEDESTRIAN
ZONE
Mon - Fri
8 am - 6.30 pm

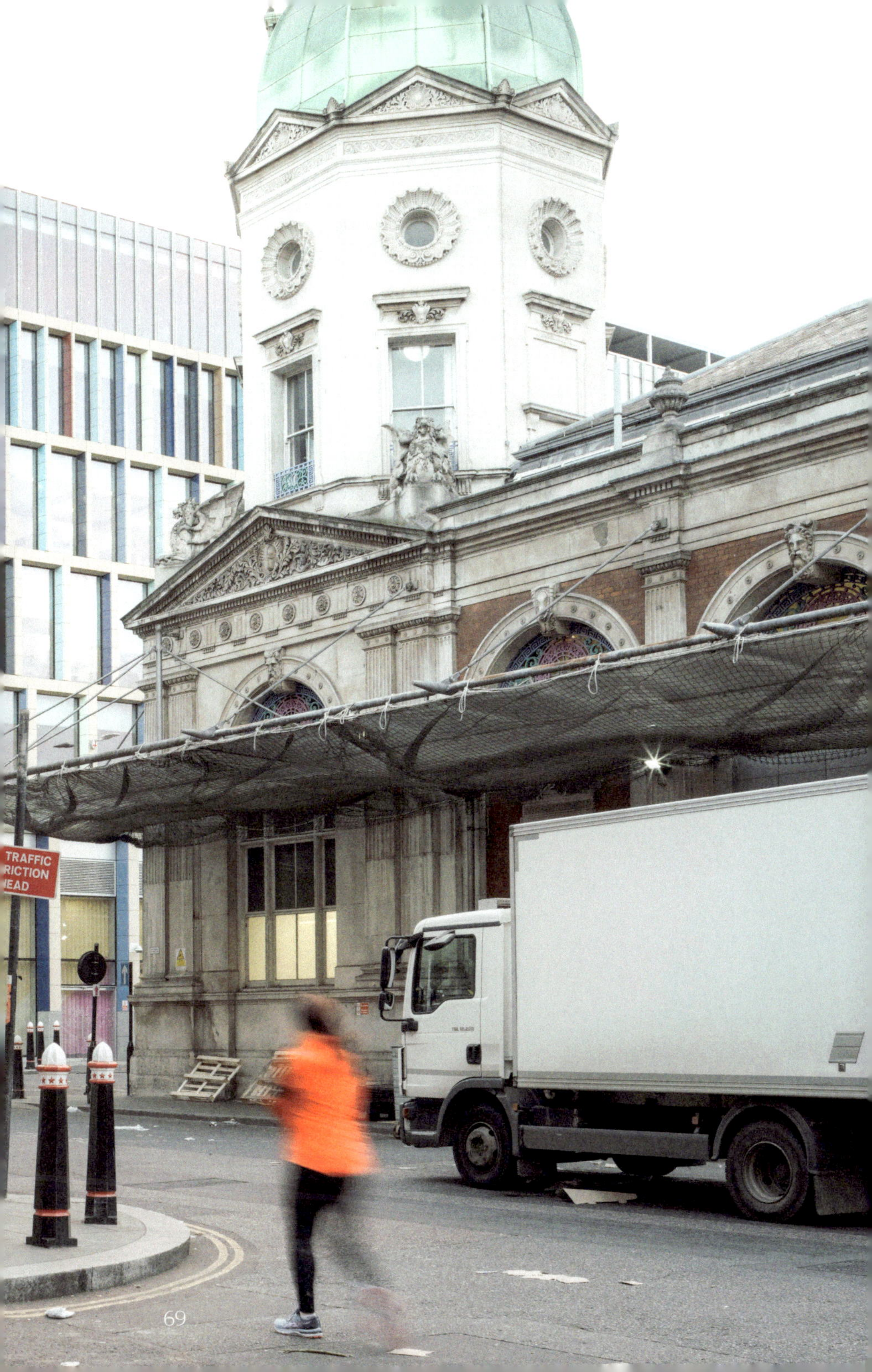
TRAFFIC
RICTION
HEAD

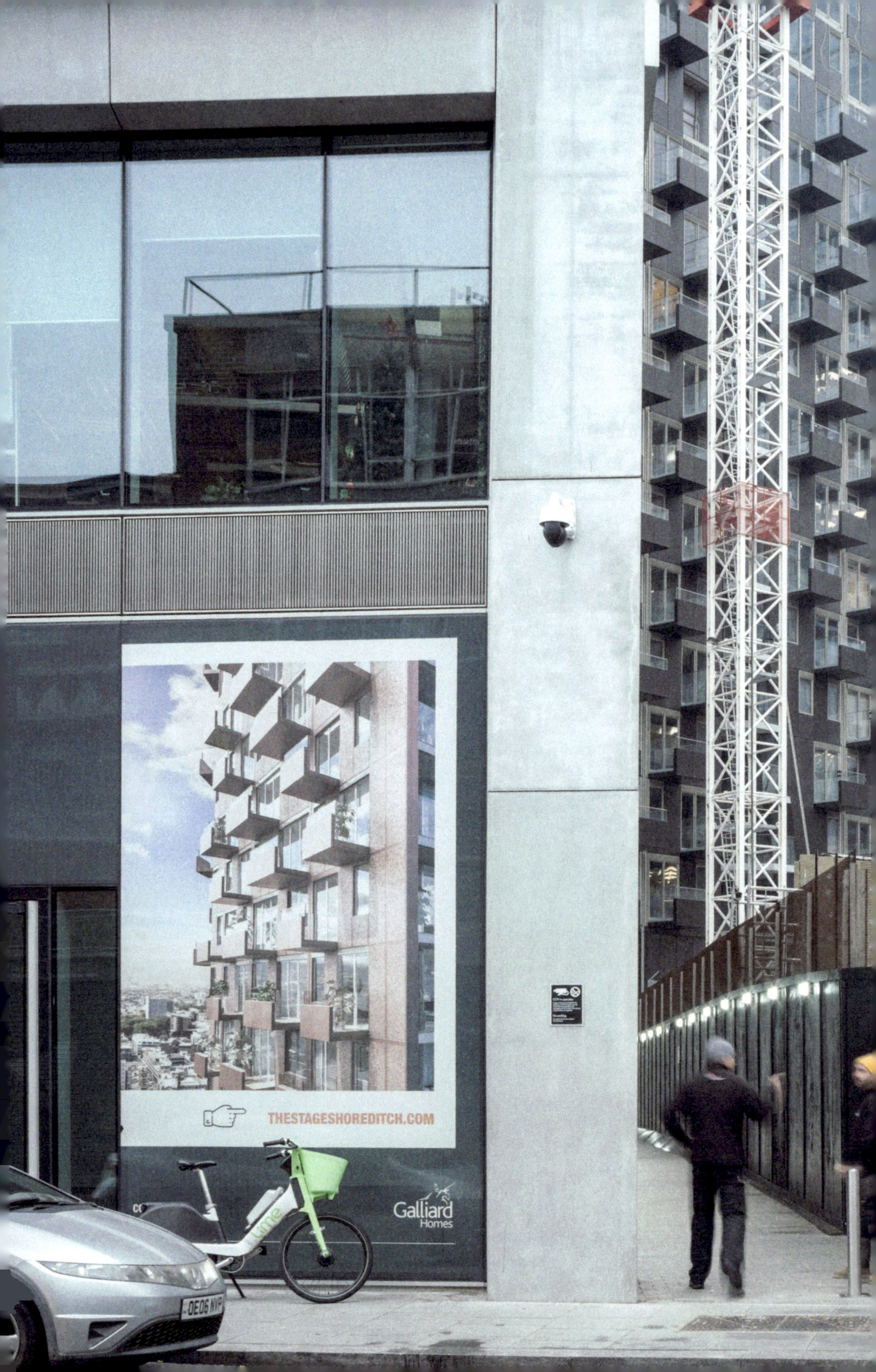
THESTAGESHOREDITCH.COM
Galliard
Homes
OE06 NVP

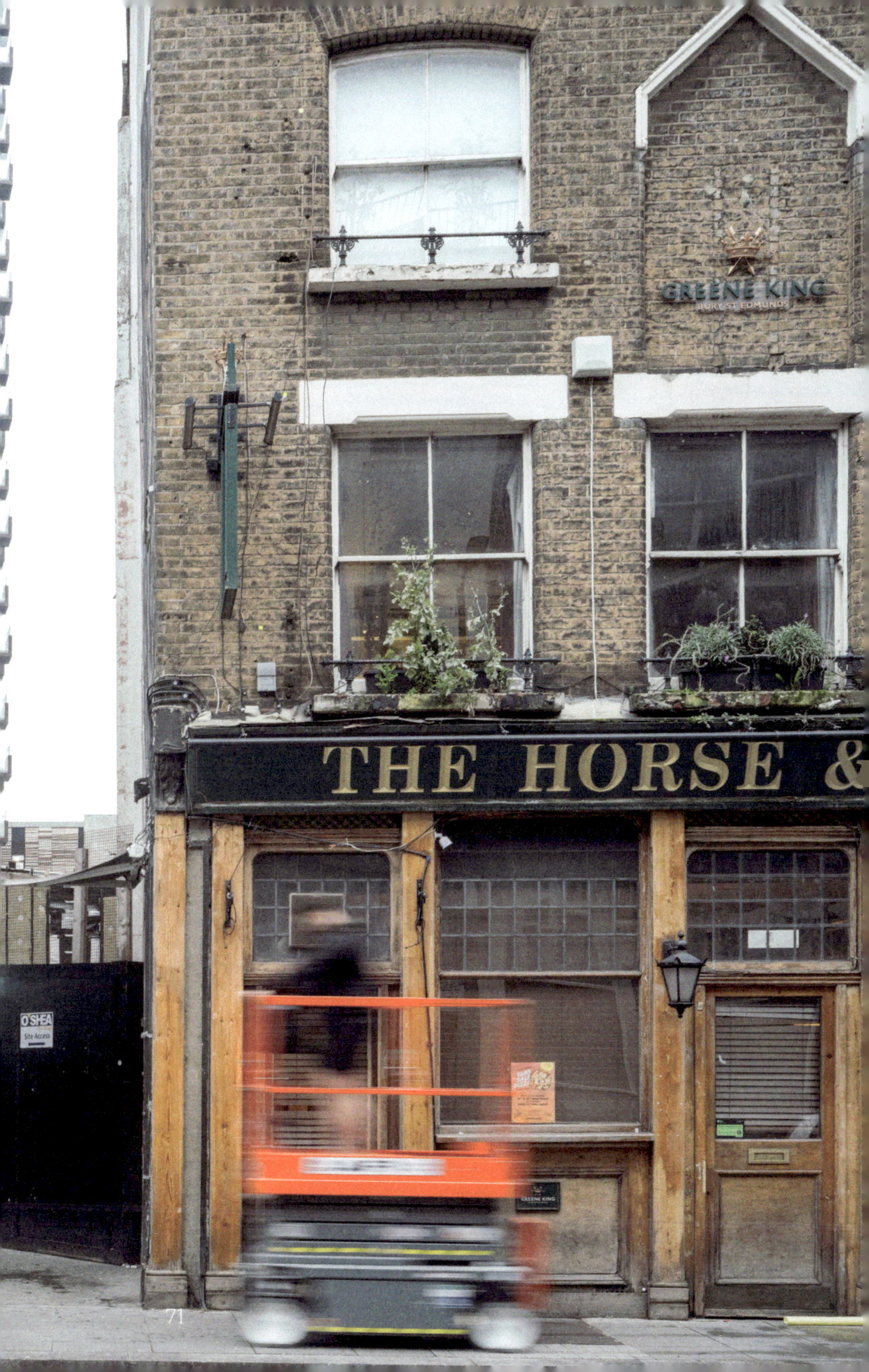
GREENE KING
BURY ST EDMUNDS
THE HORSE &
O'SHEA
Site Access
GREENE KING

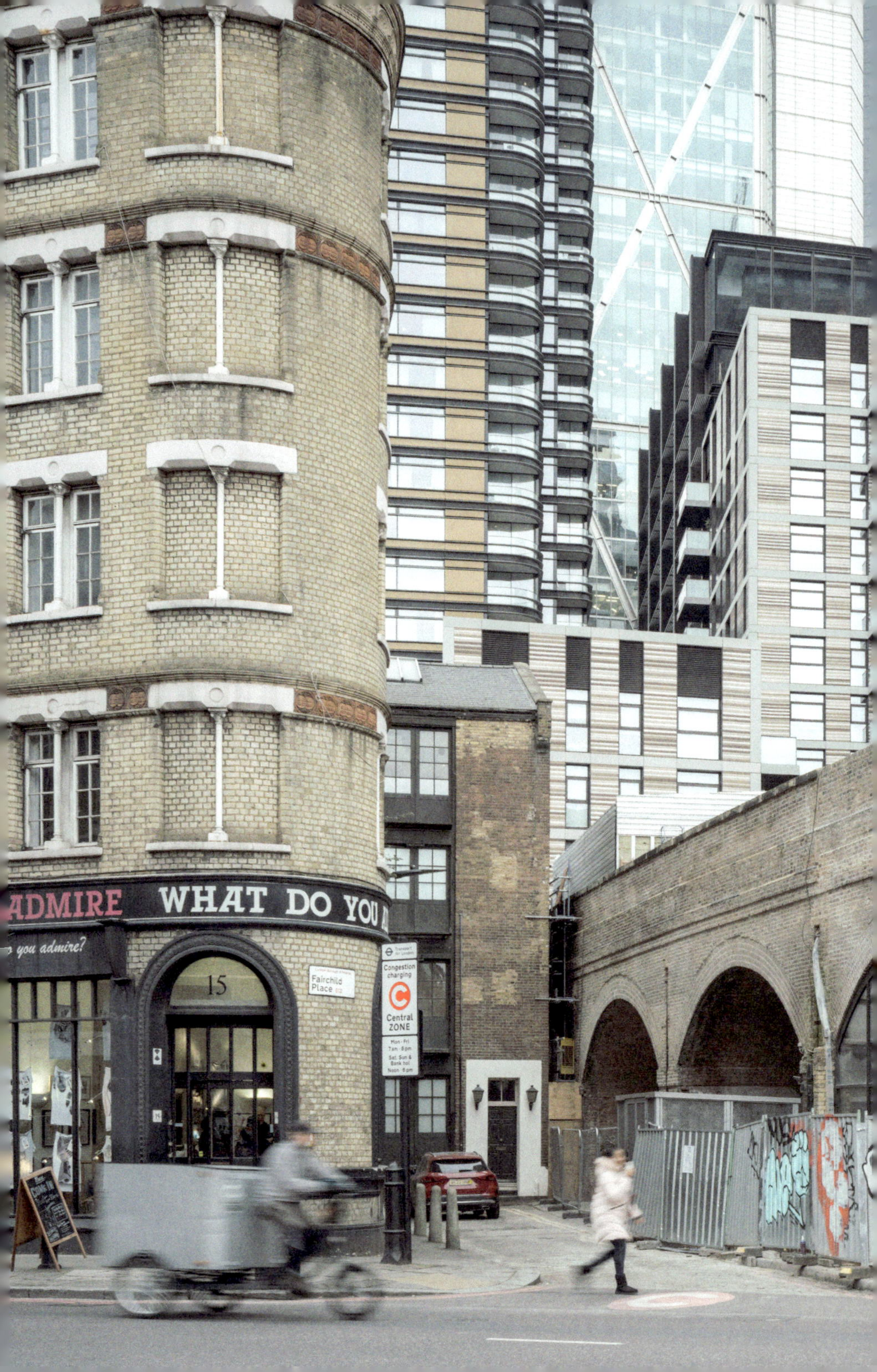
ADMIRE
WHAT DO YOU
15
Fairchild Place
Congestion charging
Central ZONE
Mon - Fri 7am - 6pm
Sat, Sun & Bank hol Noon - 6pm

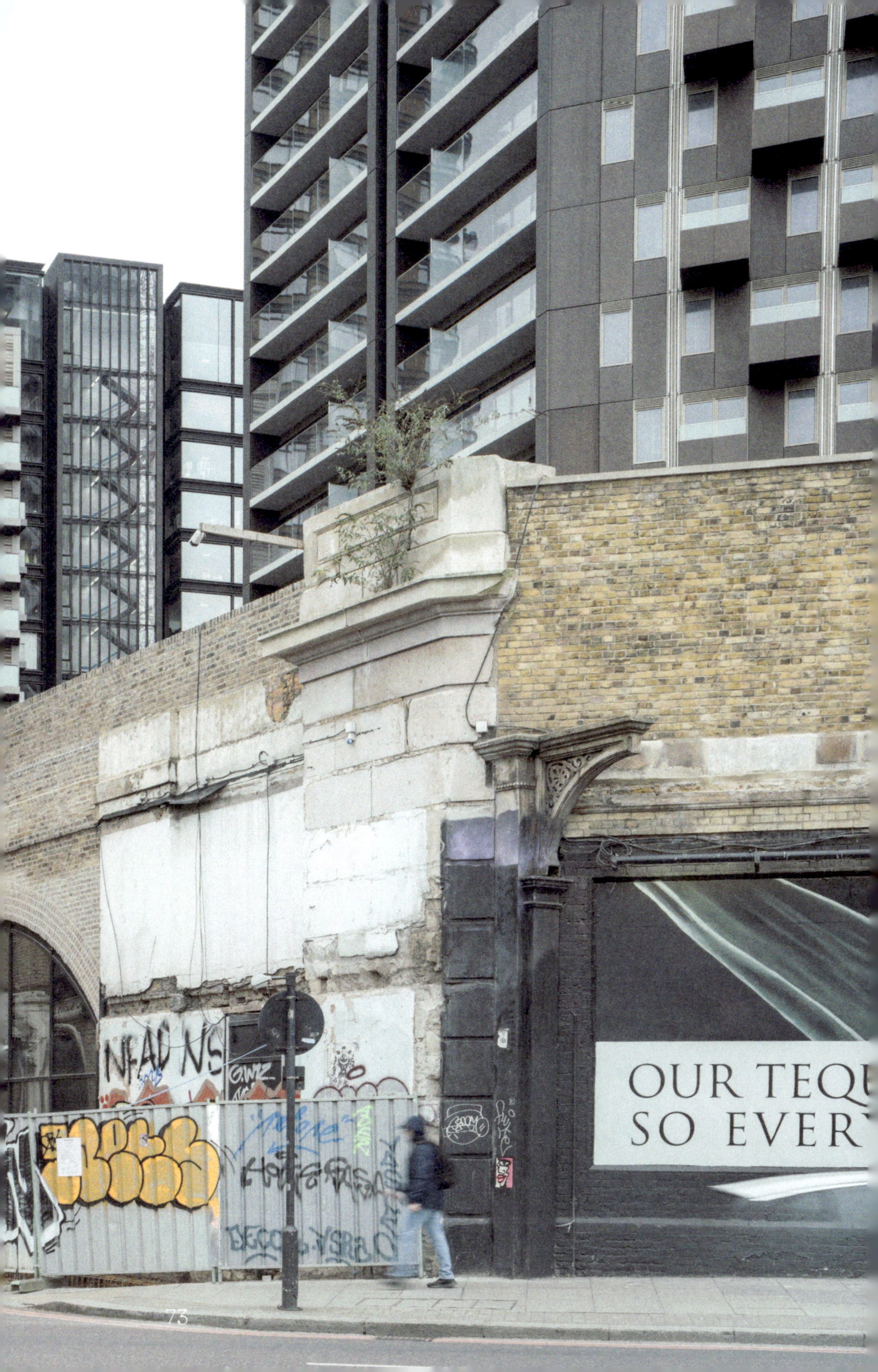
OUR TEQ
SO EVER

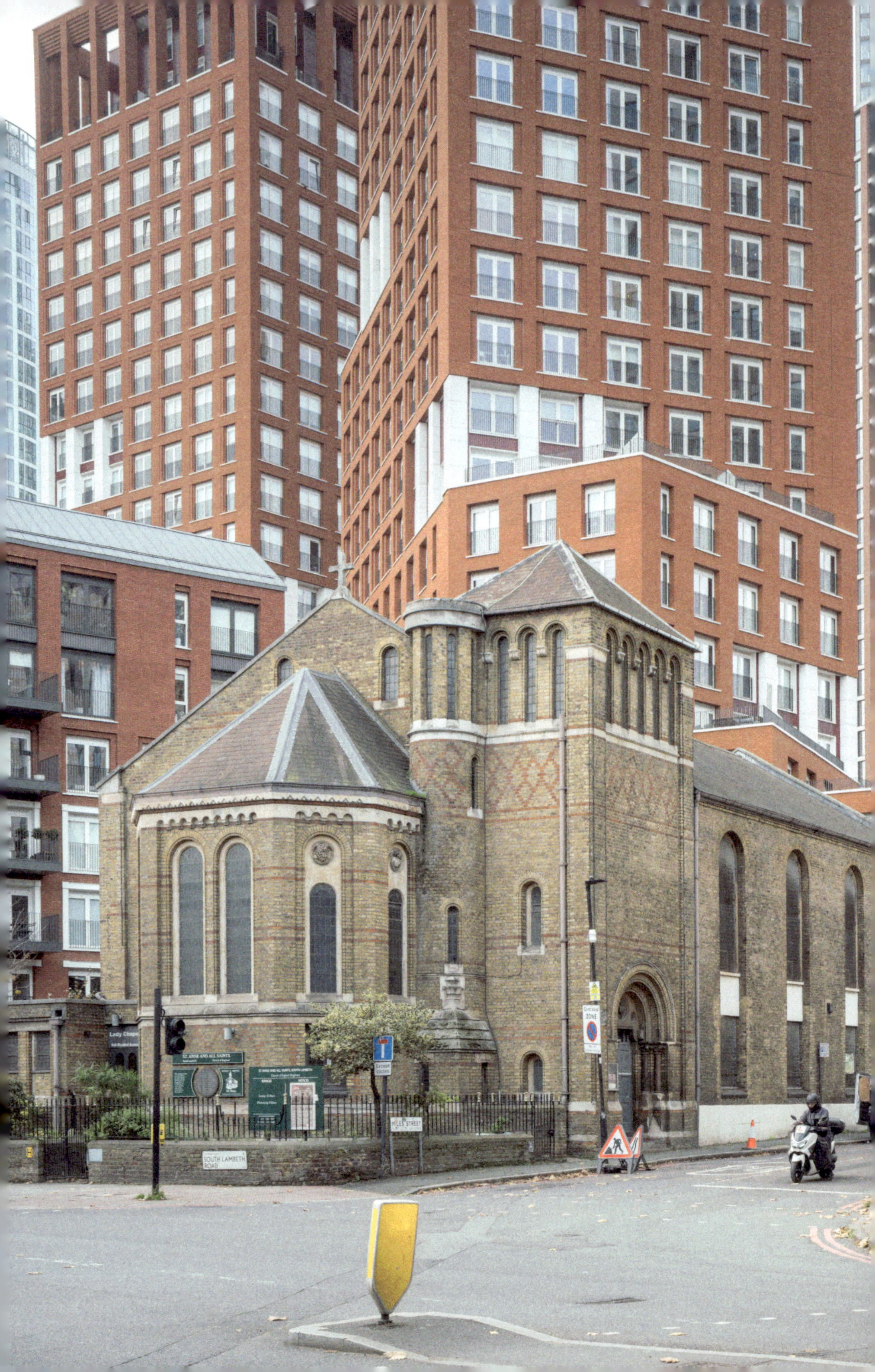
ST. ANNE AND ALL SAINTS
ST. ANNE AND ALL SAINTS, SOUTH LAMBETH
Except cycles
MILES STREET
SOUTH LAMBETH ROAD

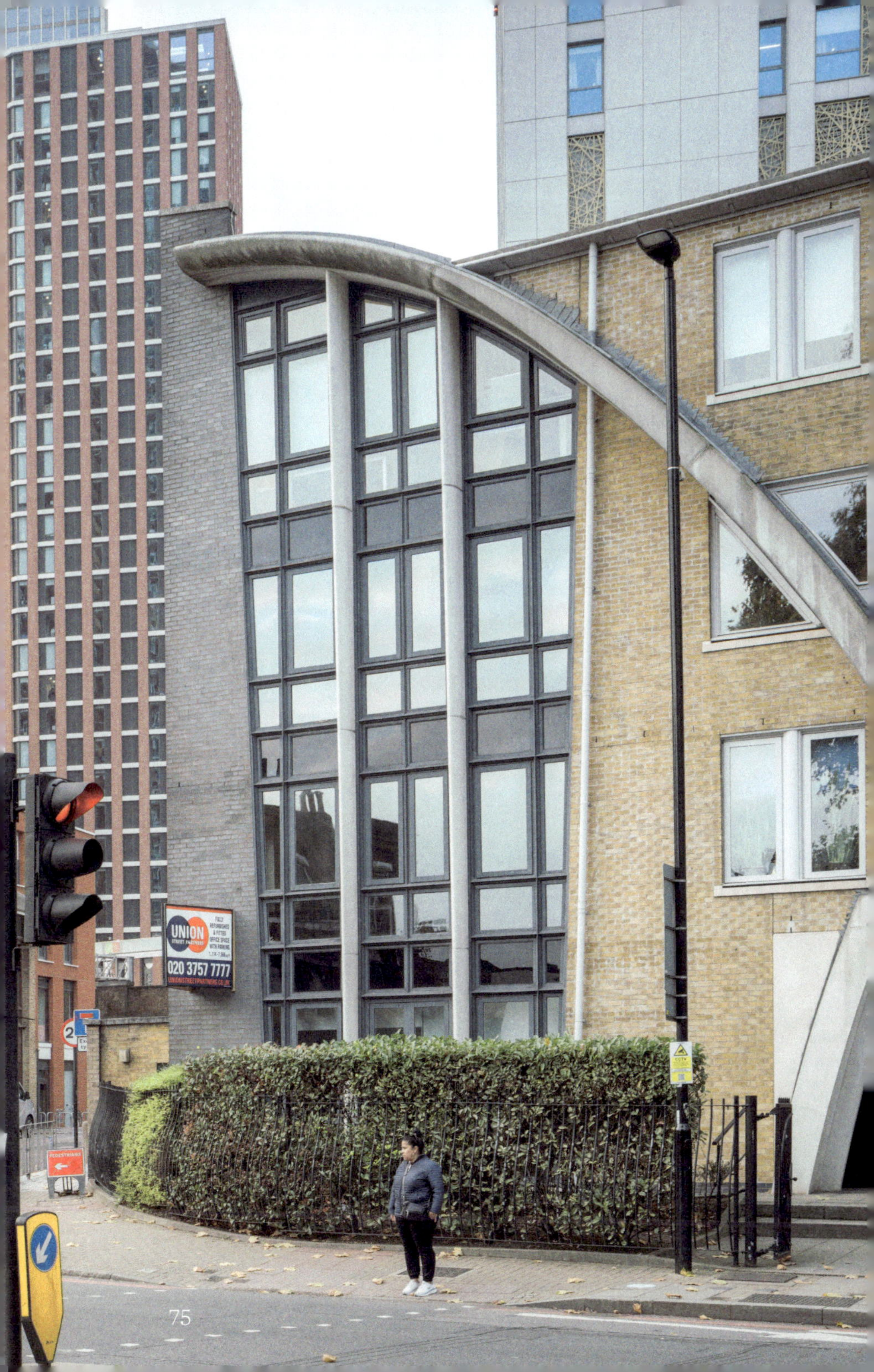
UNION
STREET PARTNERS
FULLY
REFURBISHED
& FITTED
OFFICE SPACE
WITH PARKING
020 3757 7777
UNIONSTREETPARTNERS.CO.UK
PEDESTRIANS

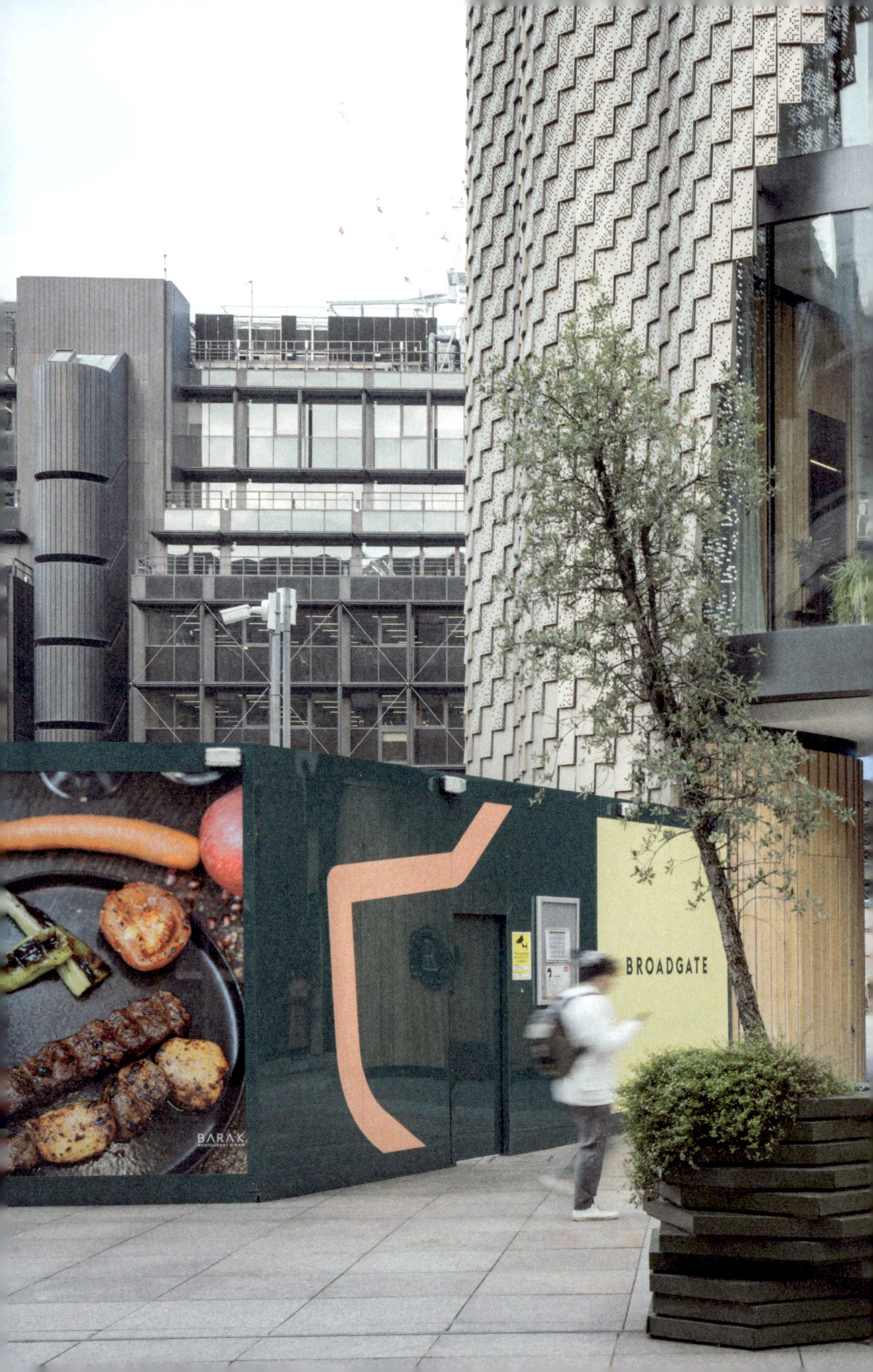
BROADGATE
BARAK

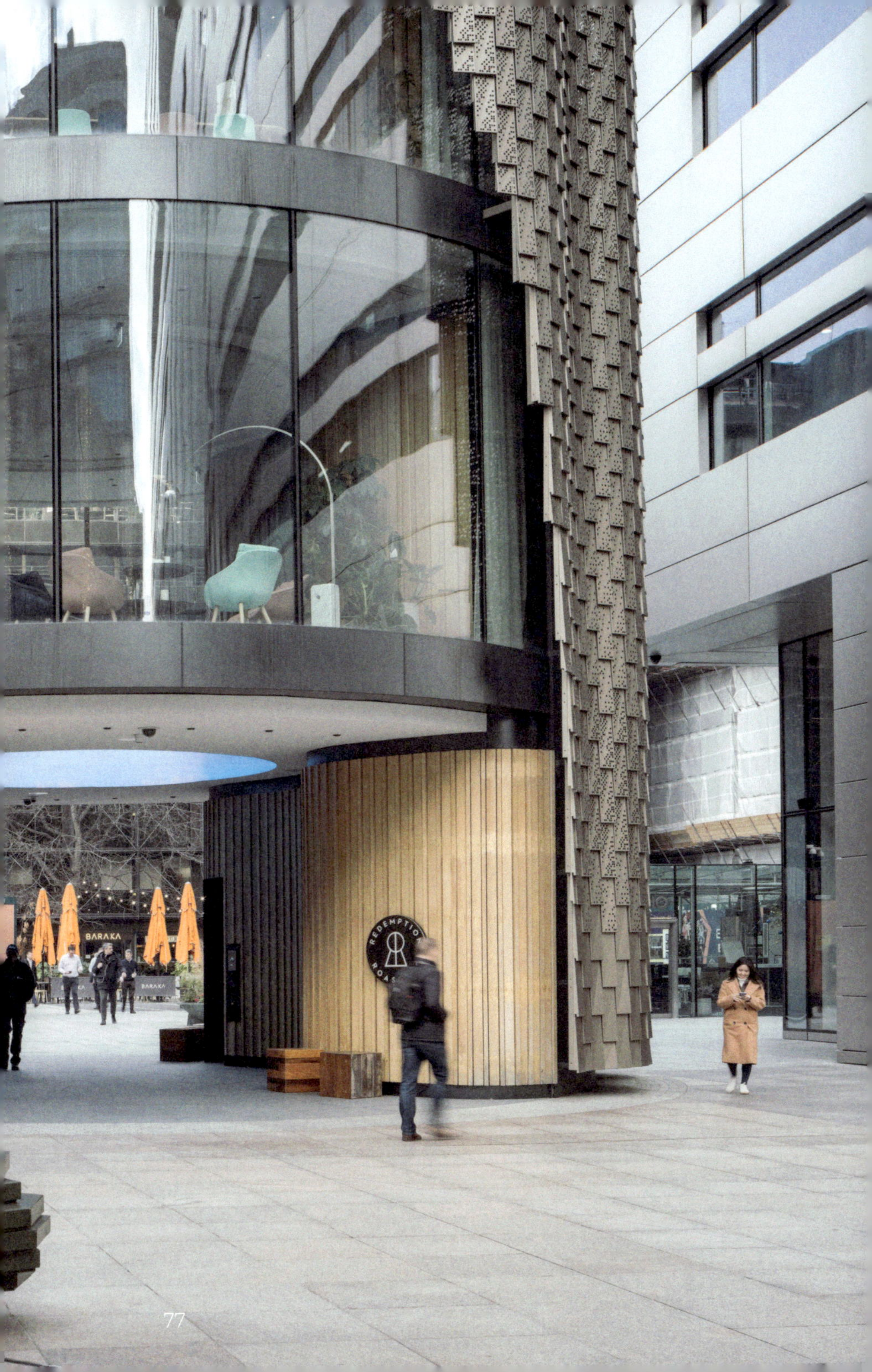
BARAKA

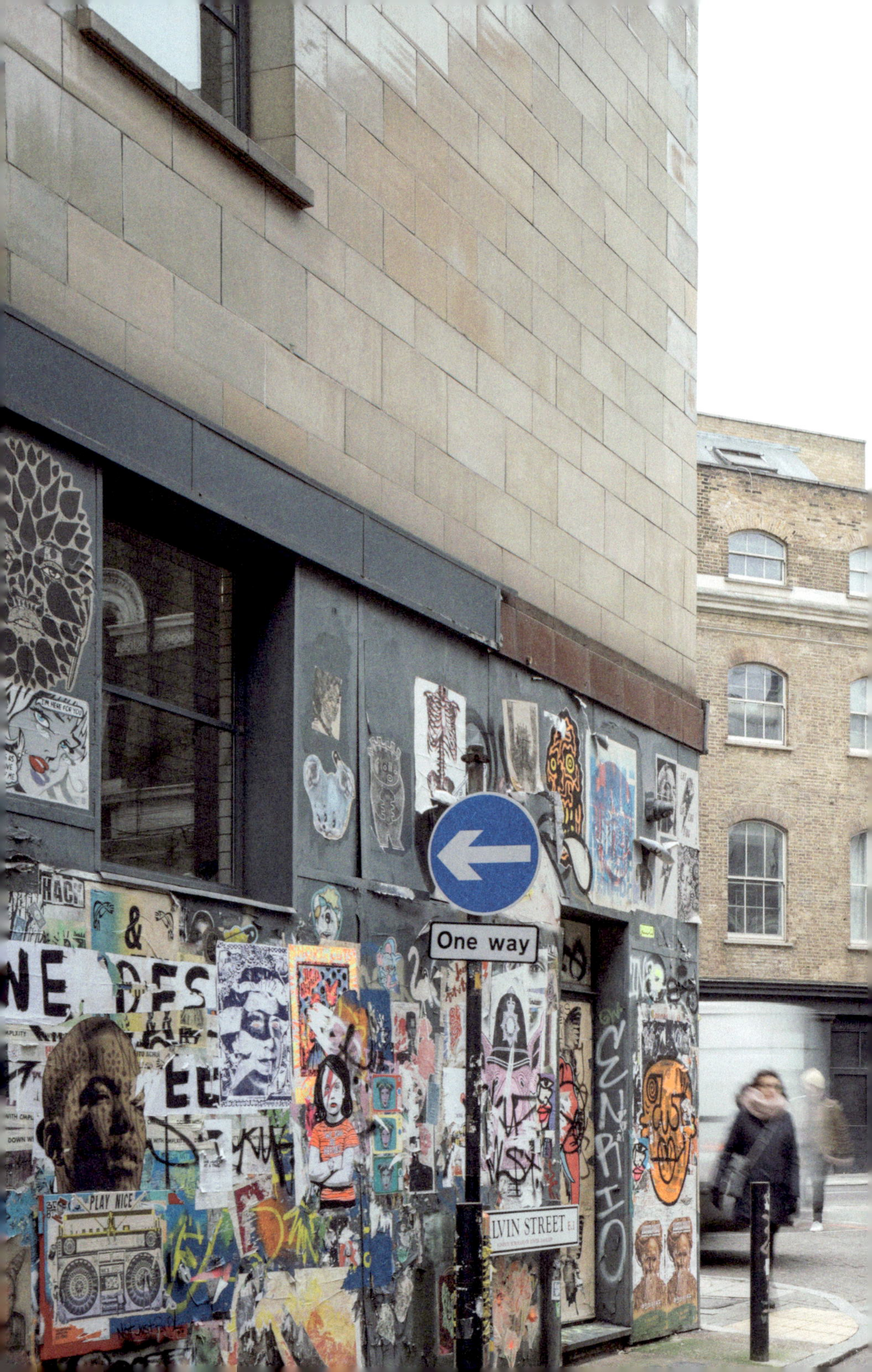
One way
LVIN STREET E1
HACK
PLAY NICE

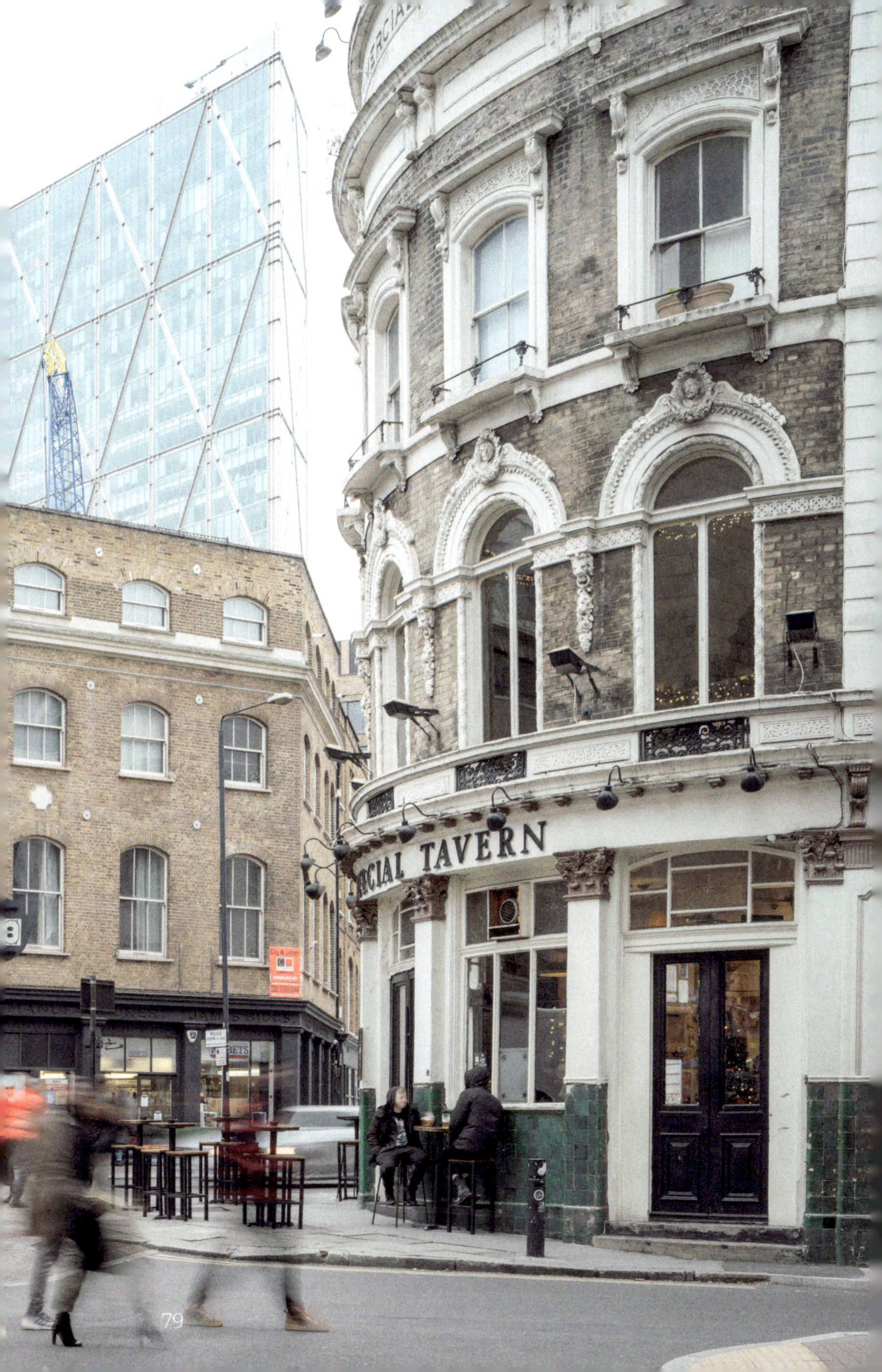
RCIAL TAVERN

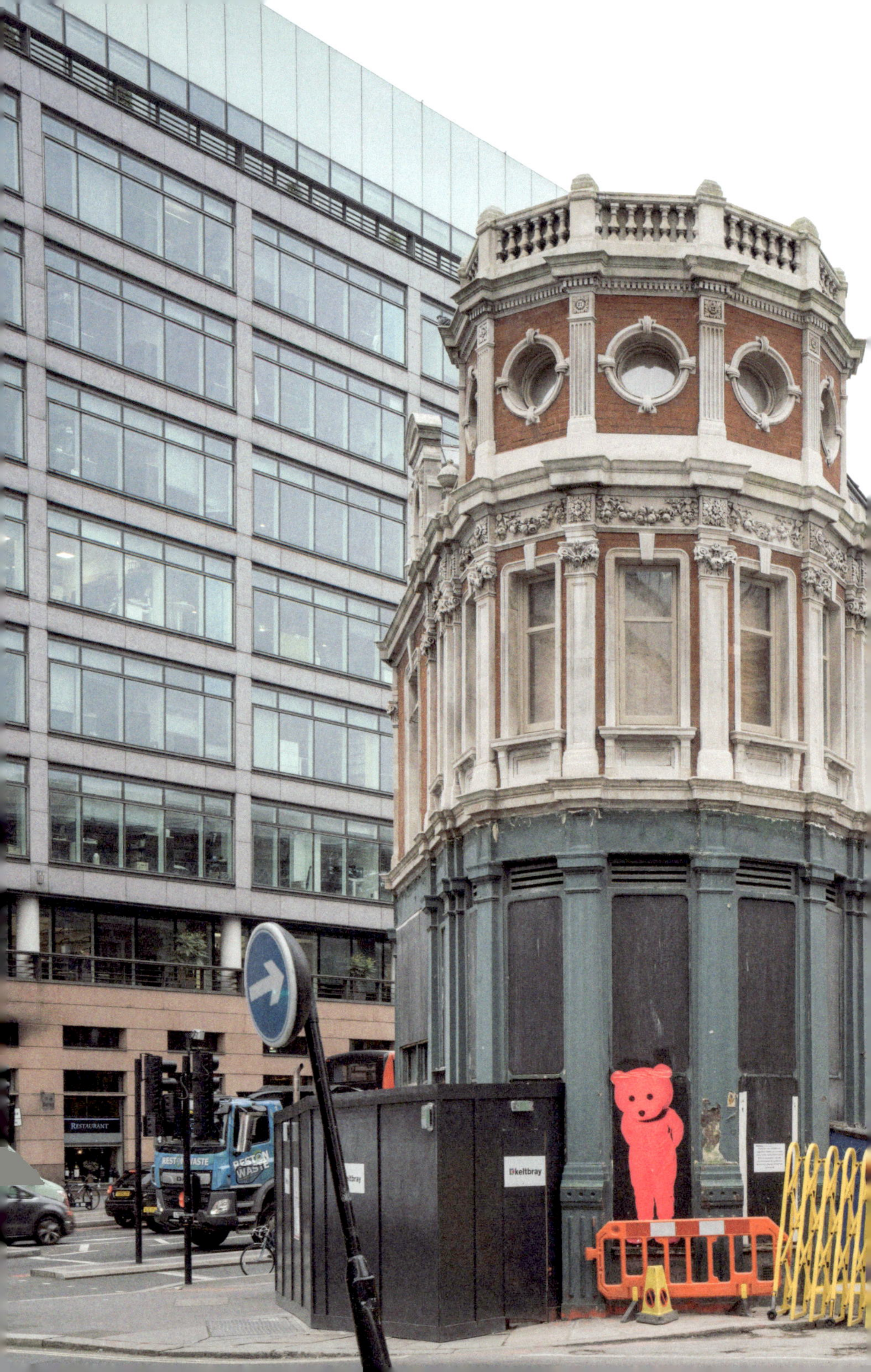
RESTAURANT
RESTON WASTE
keltbray

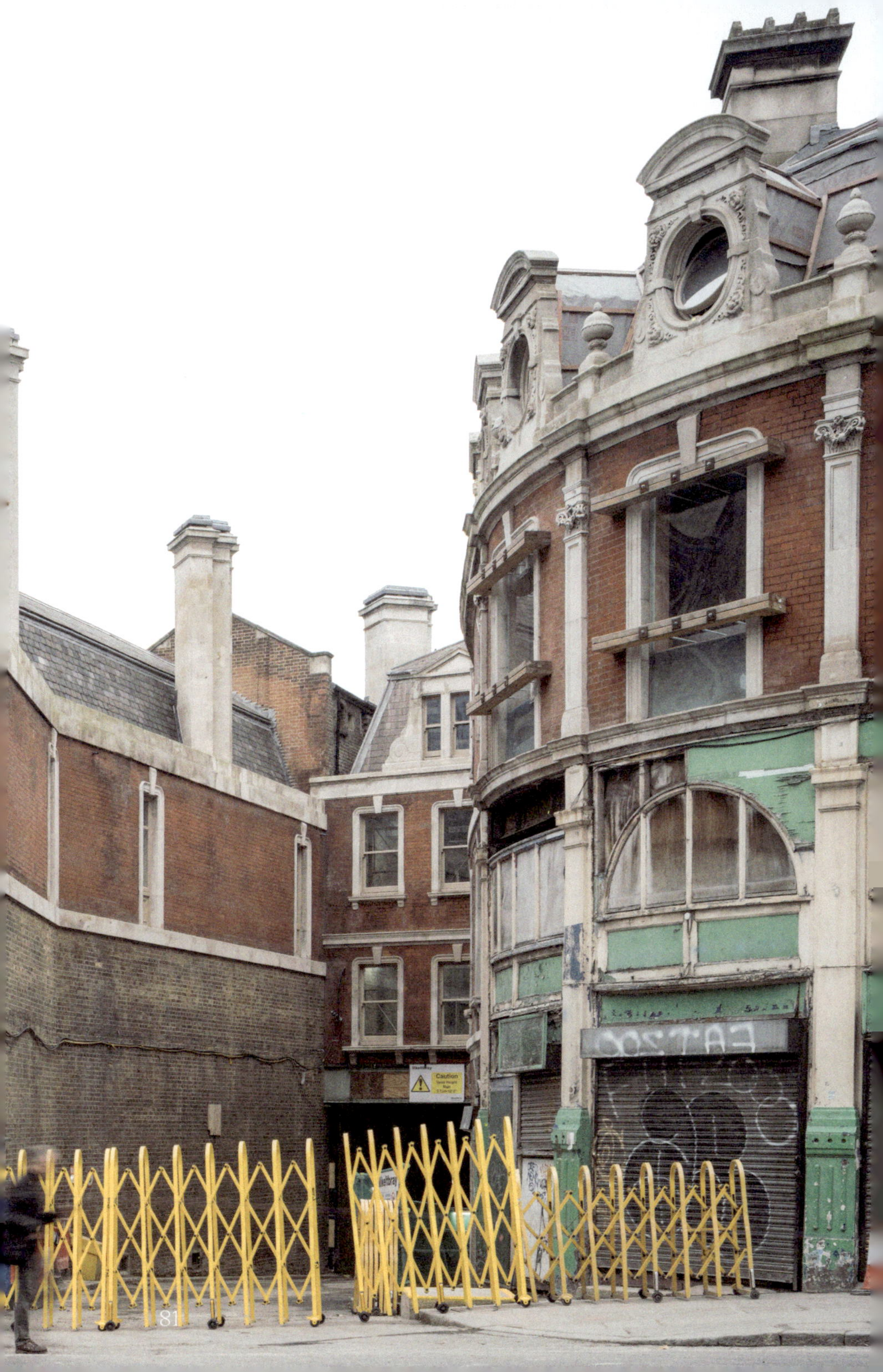
Caution

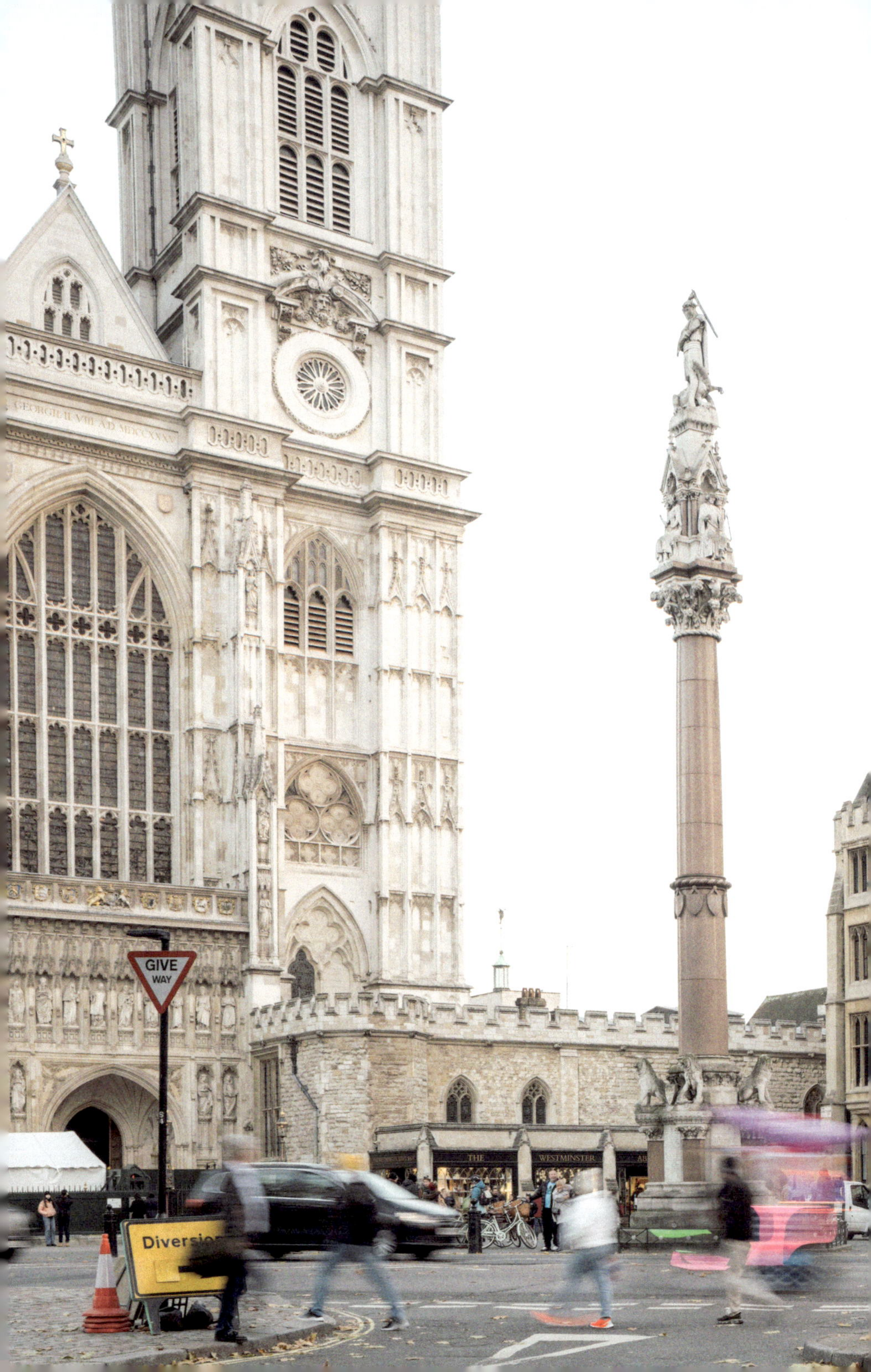
GIVE
WAY
THE
WESTMINSTER

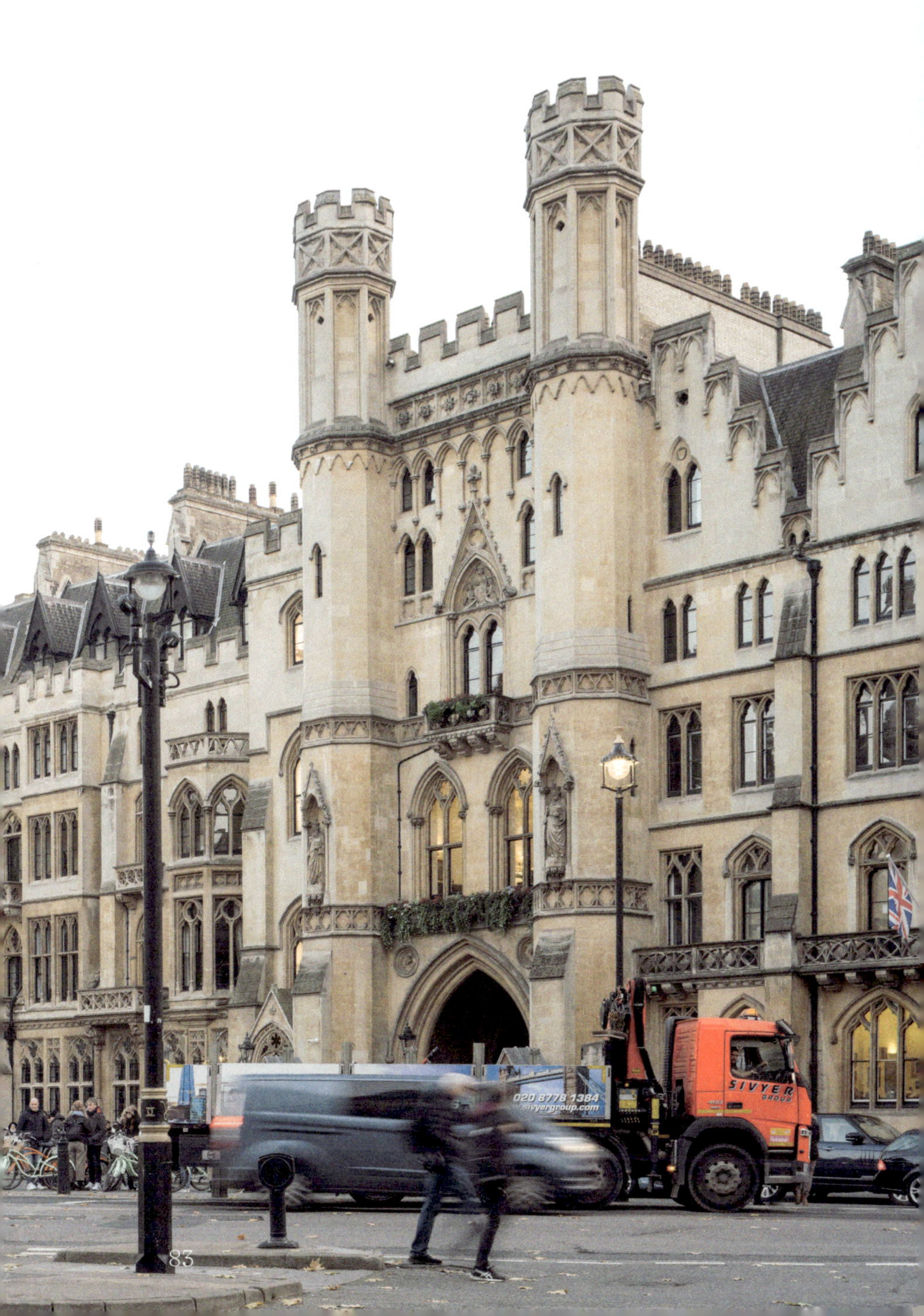
SIVYER
020 8778 1384

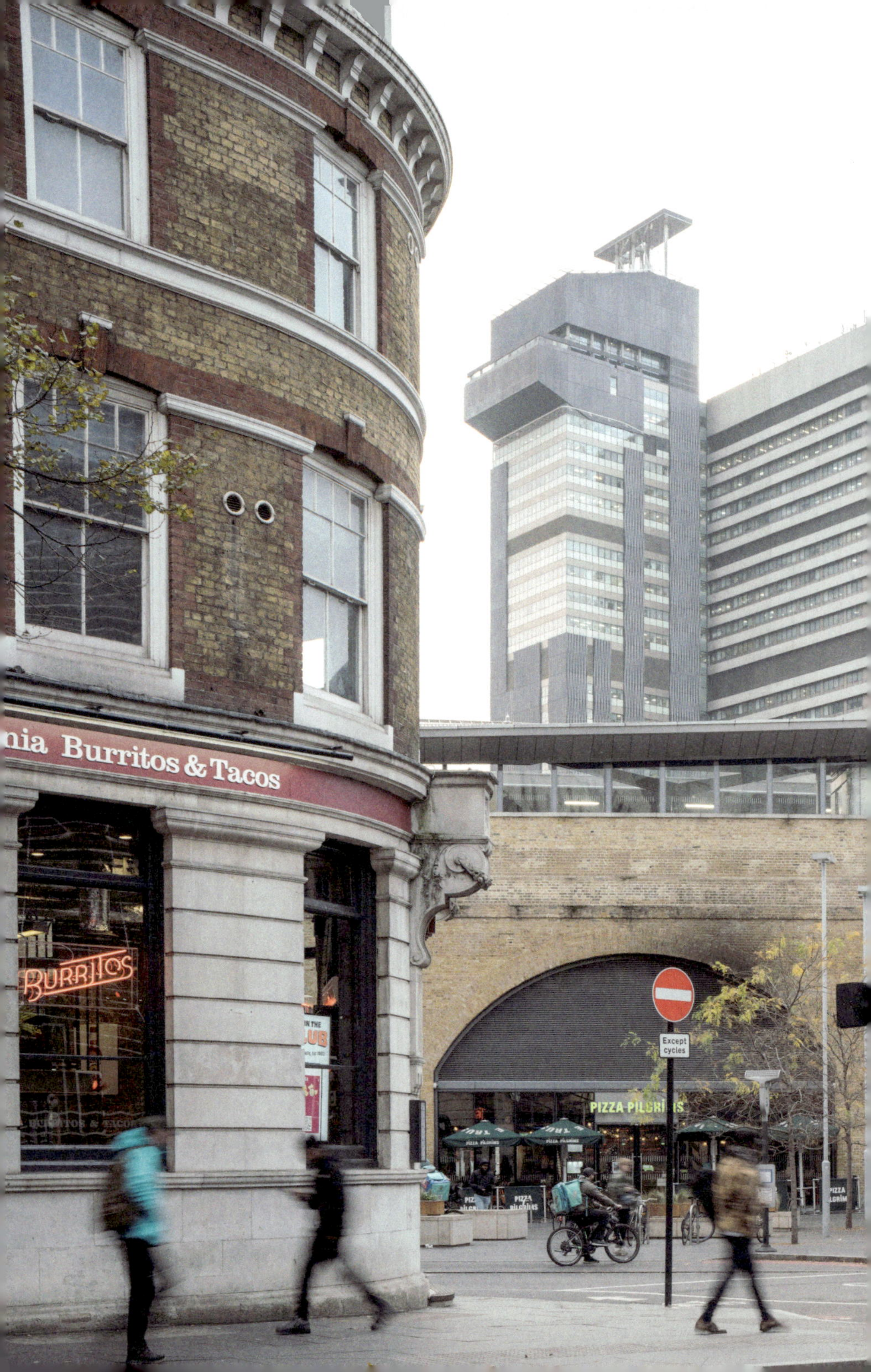
nia Burritos & Tacos
BURRITOS
Except cycles

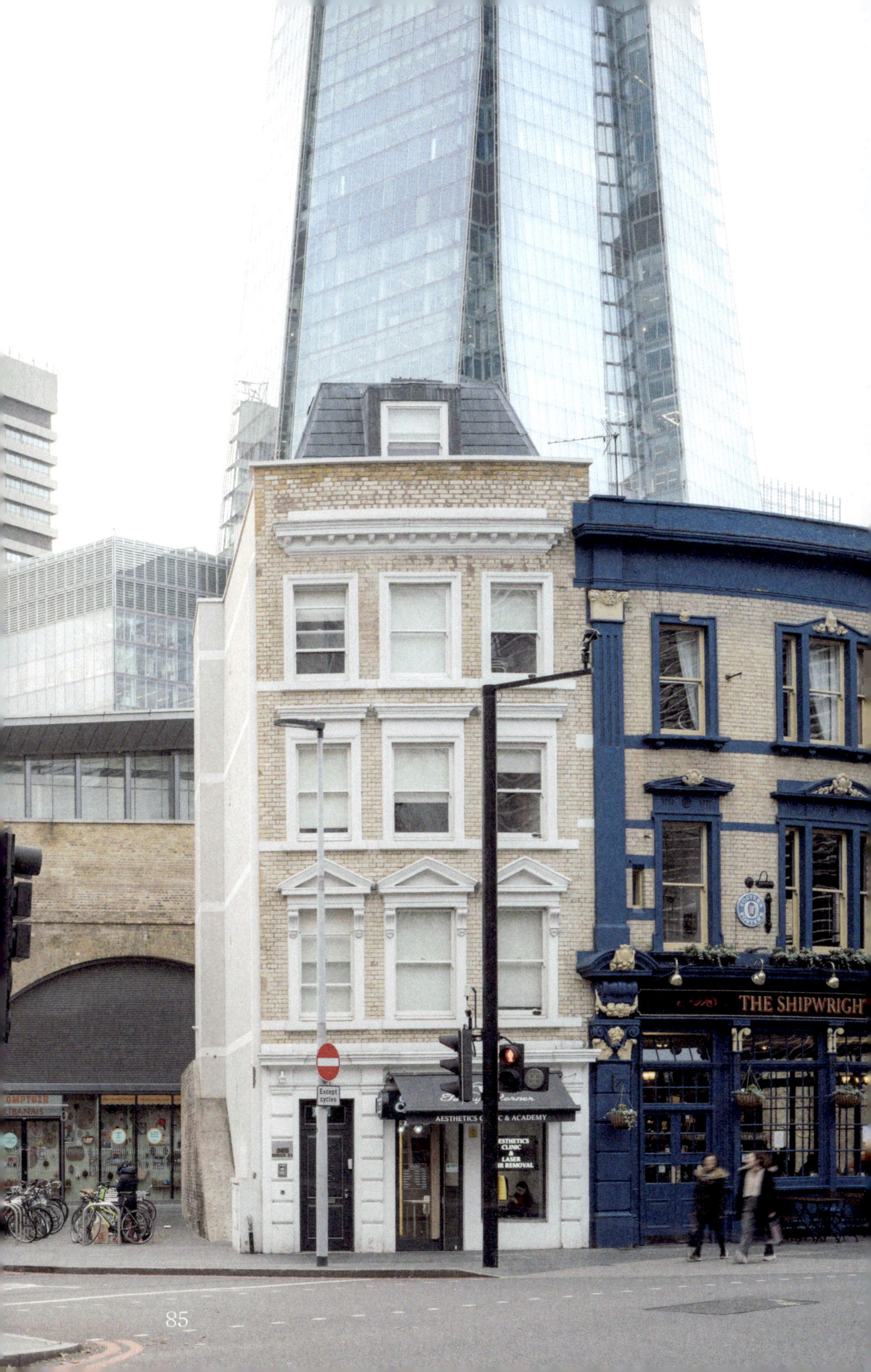
THE SHIPWRIGH
Except cycles
AESTHETICS CLINIC & LASER

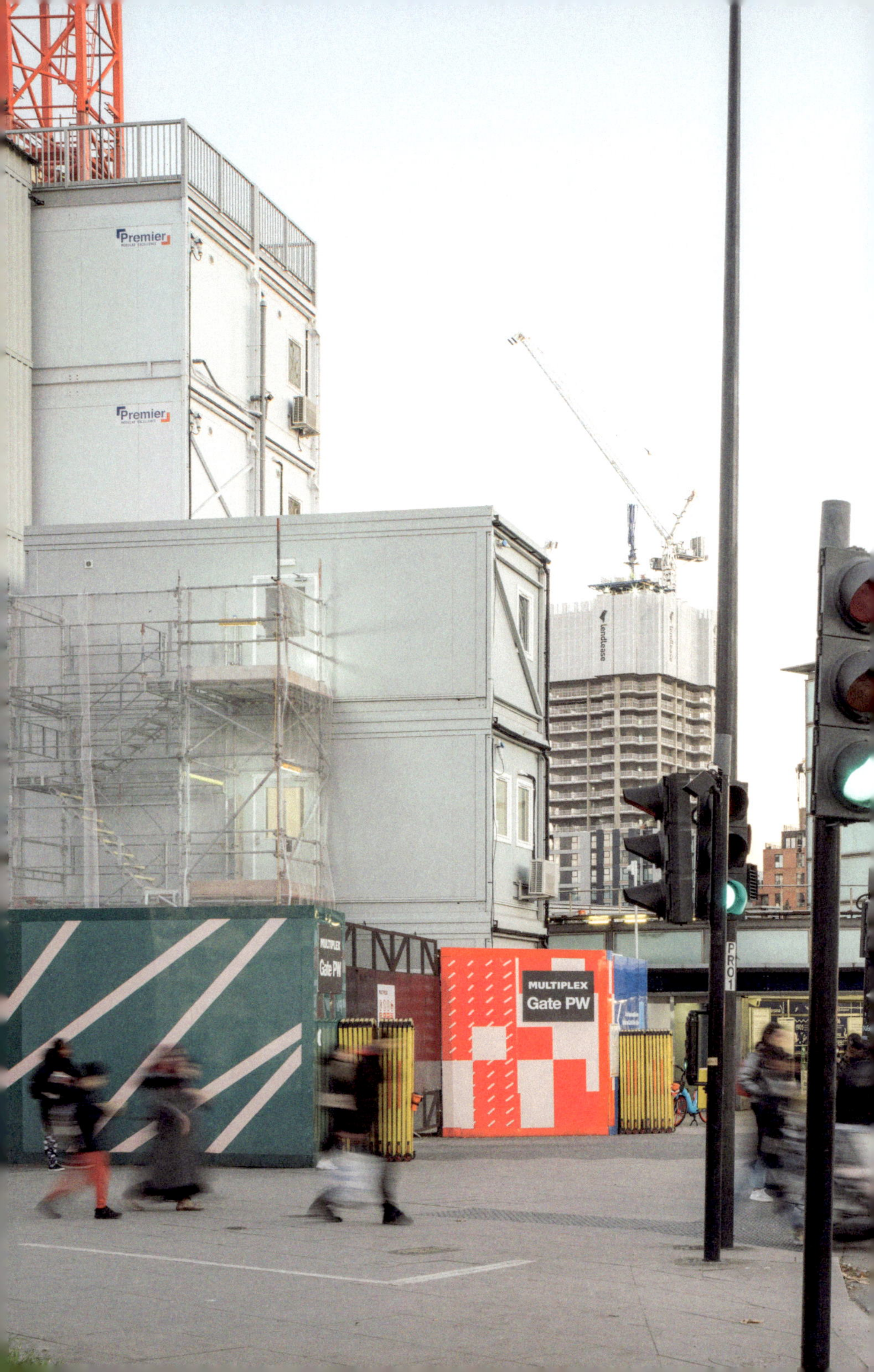
Premier
Premier
MULTIPLEX
Gate PW
MULTIPLEX
Gate PW
lendlease
PR01

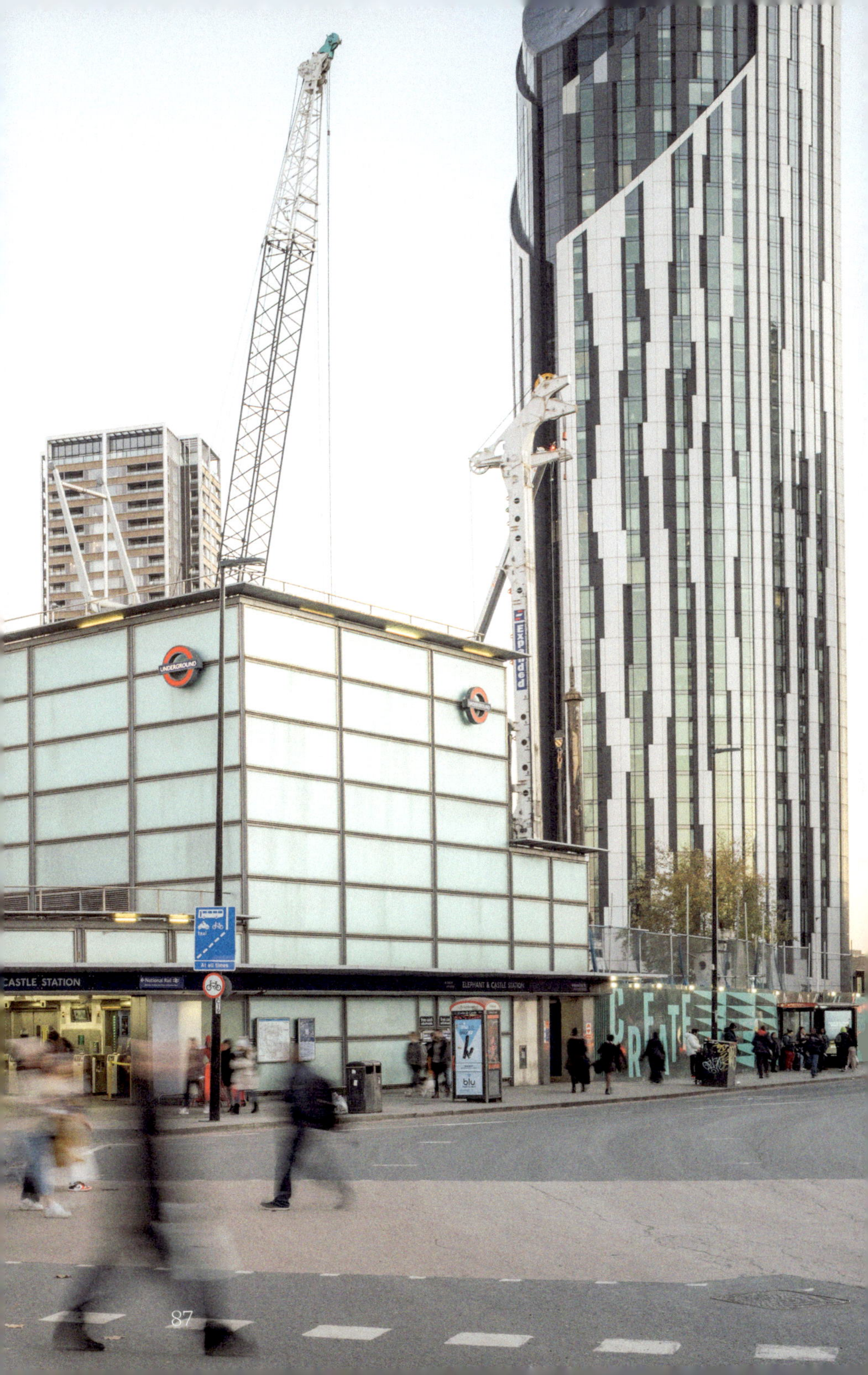
UNDERGROUND
CASTLE STATION
National Rail
ELEPHANT & CASTLE STATION
At all times
blu

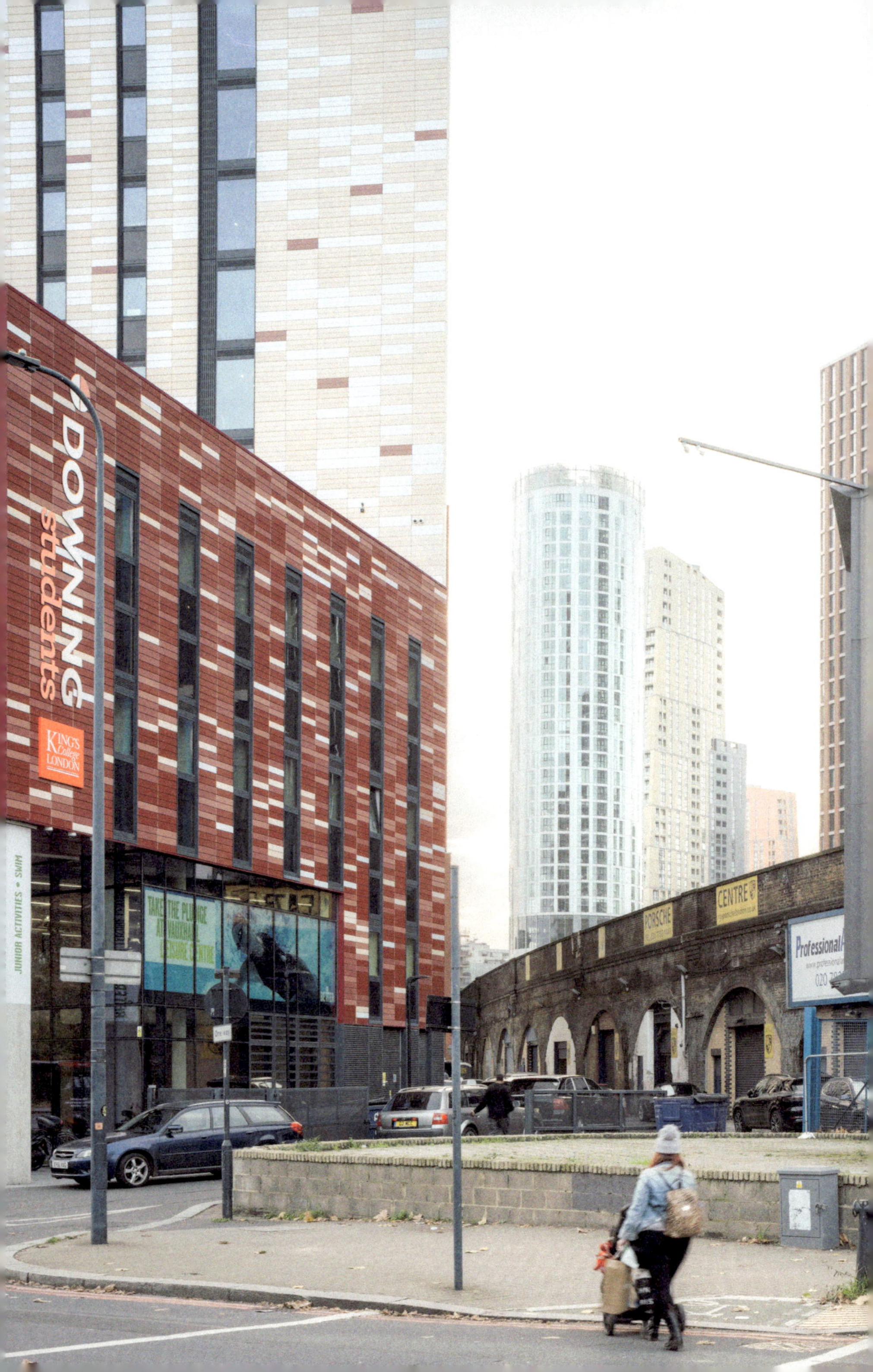
DOWNING
students
KING'S College LONDON
TAKE THE PLUNGE
JUNIOR ACTIVITIES • SWIM
PORSCHE
CENTRE
Professional

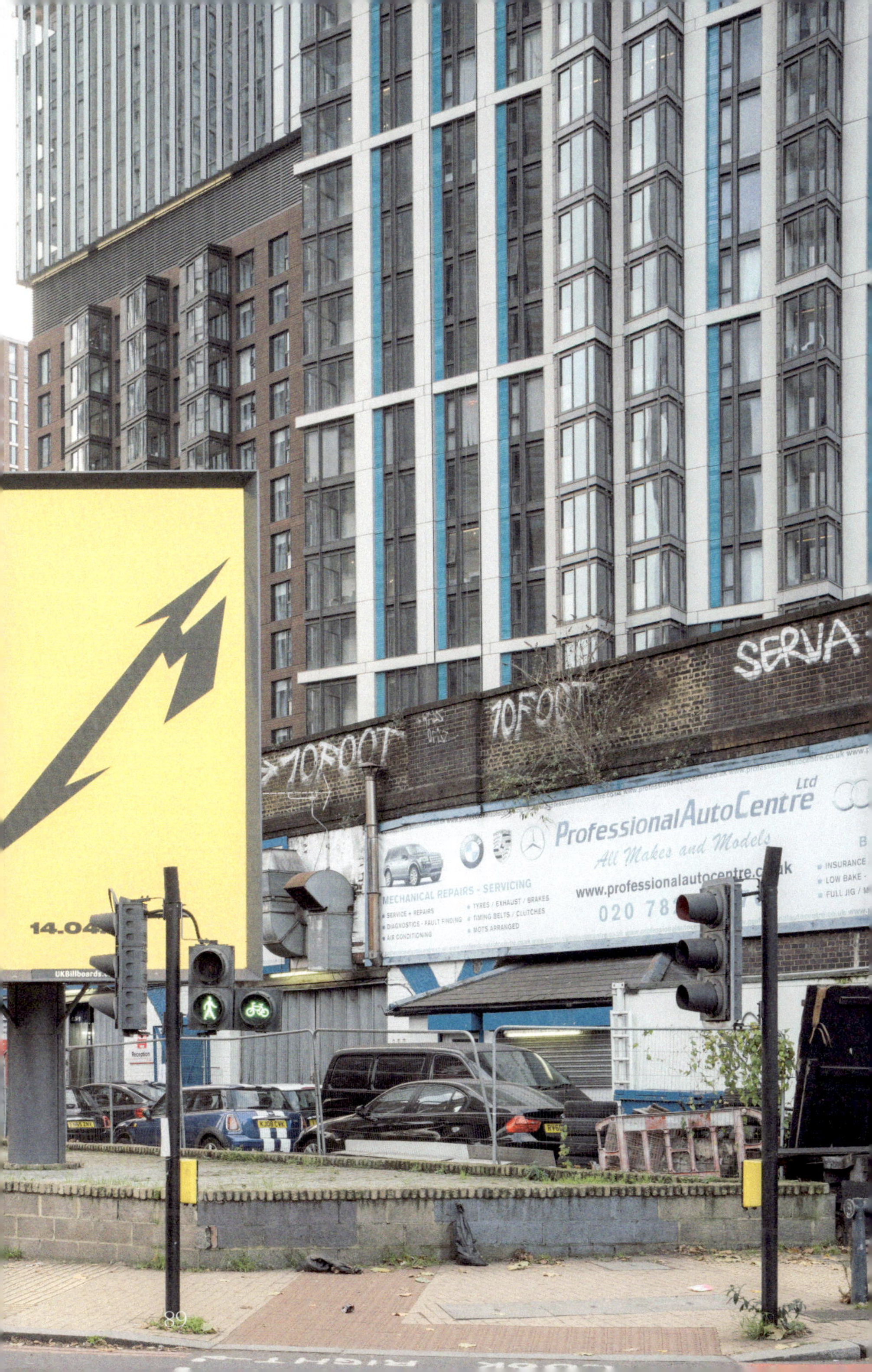
SERVA
10FOOT
10FOOT
ProfessionalAutoCentre Ltd
All Makes and Models
www.professionalautocentre.co.uk
MECHANICAL REPAIRS - SERVICING
SERVICE + REPAIRS
DIAGNOSTICS - FAULT FINDING
AIR CONDITIONING
TYRES / EXHAUST / BRAKES
TIMING BELTS / CLUTCHES
MOTS ARRANGED
INSURANCE

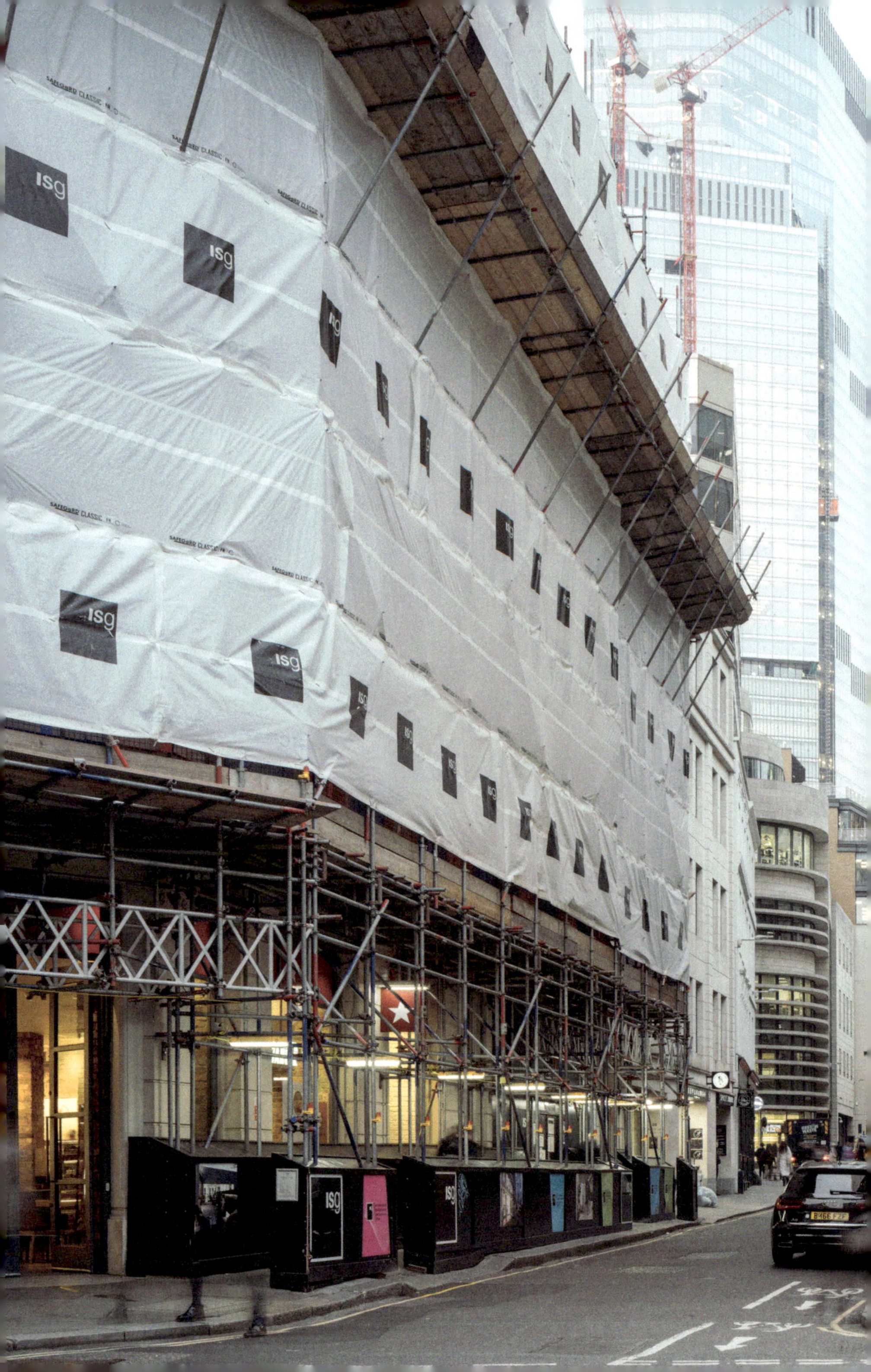
isg

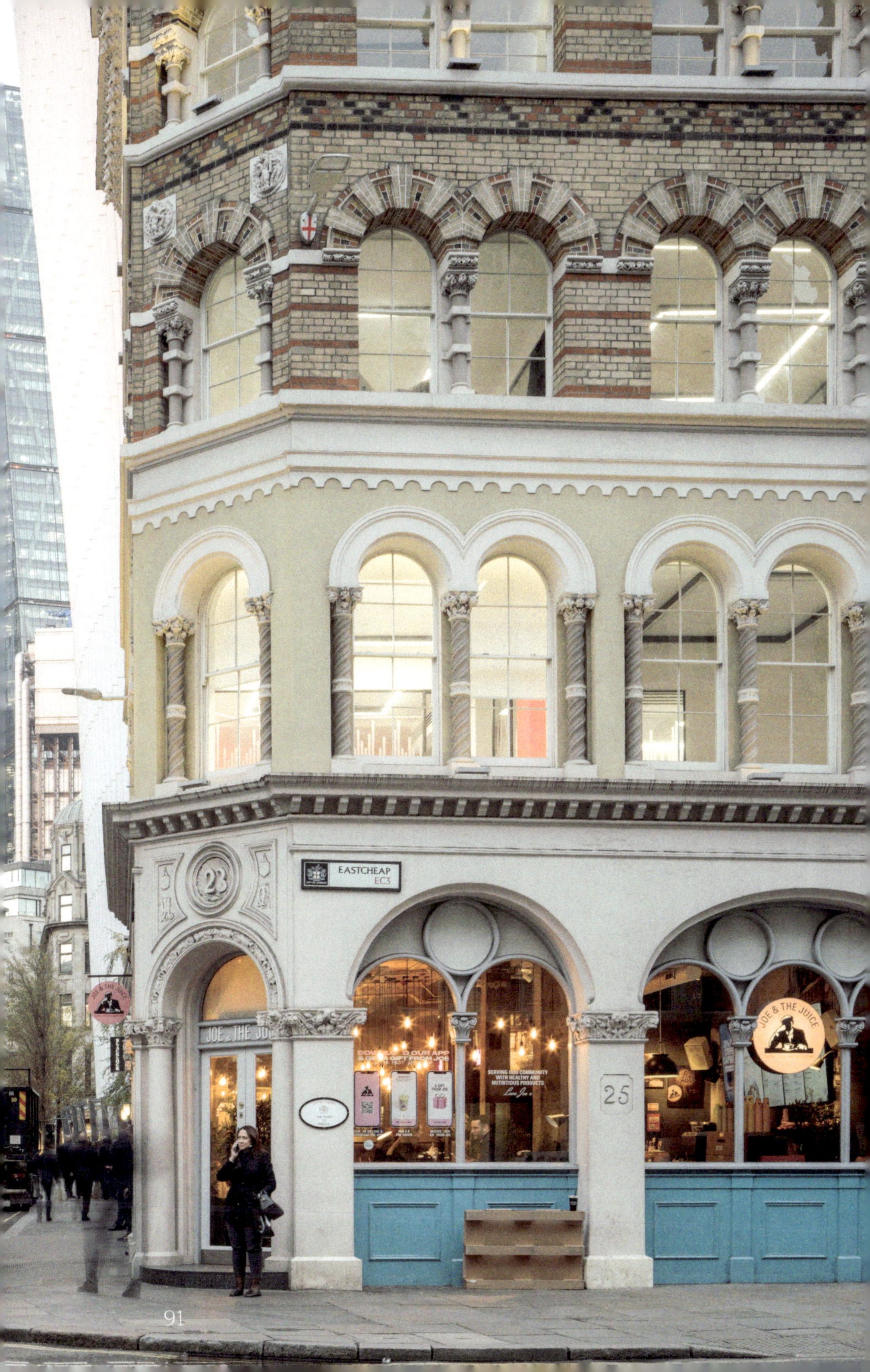
EASTCHEAP
EC3
23
25
JOE & THE JUICE

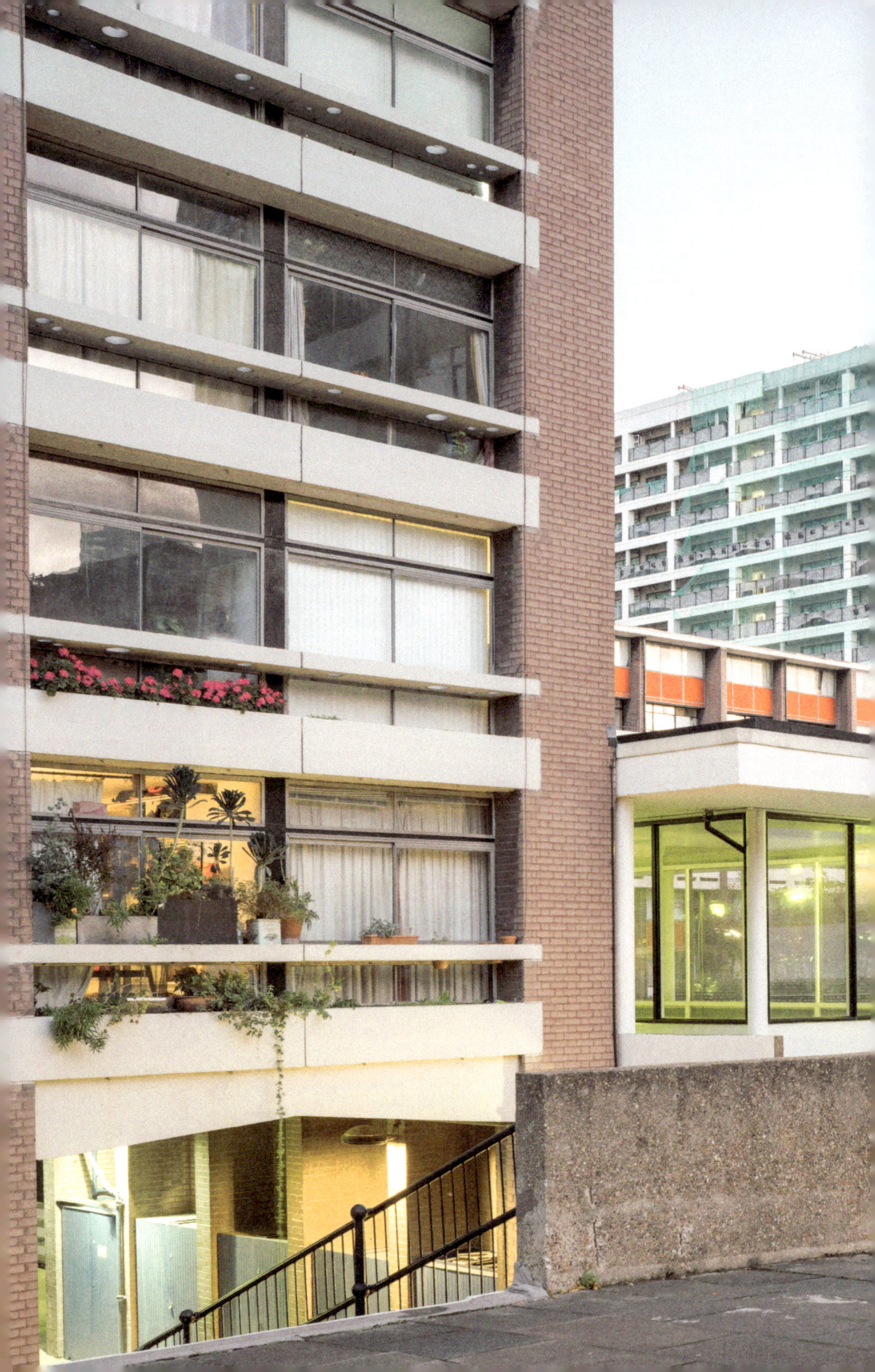

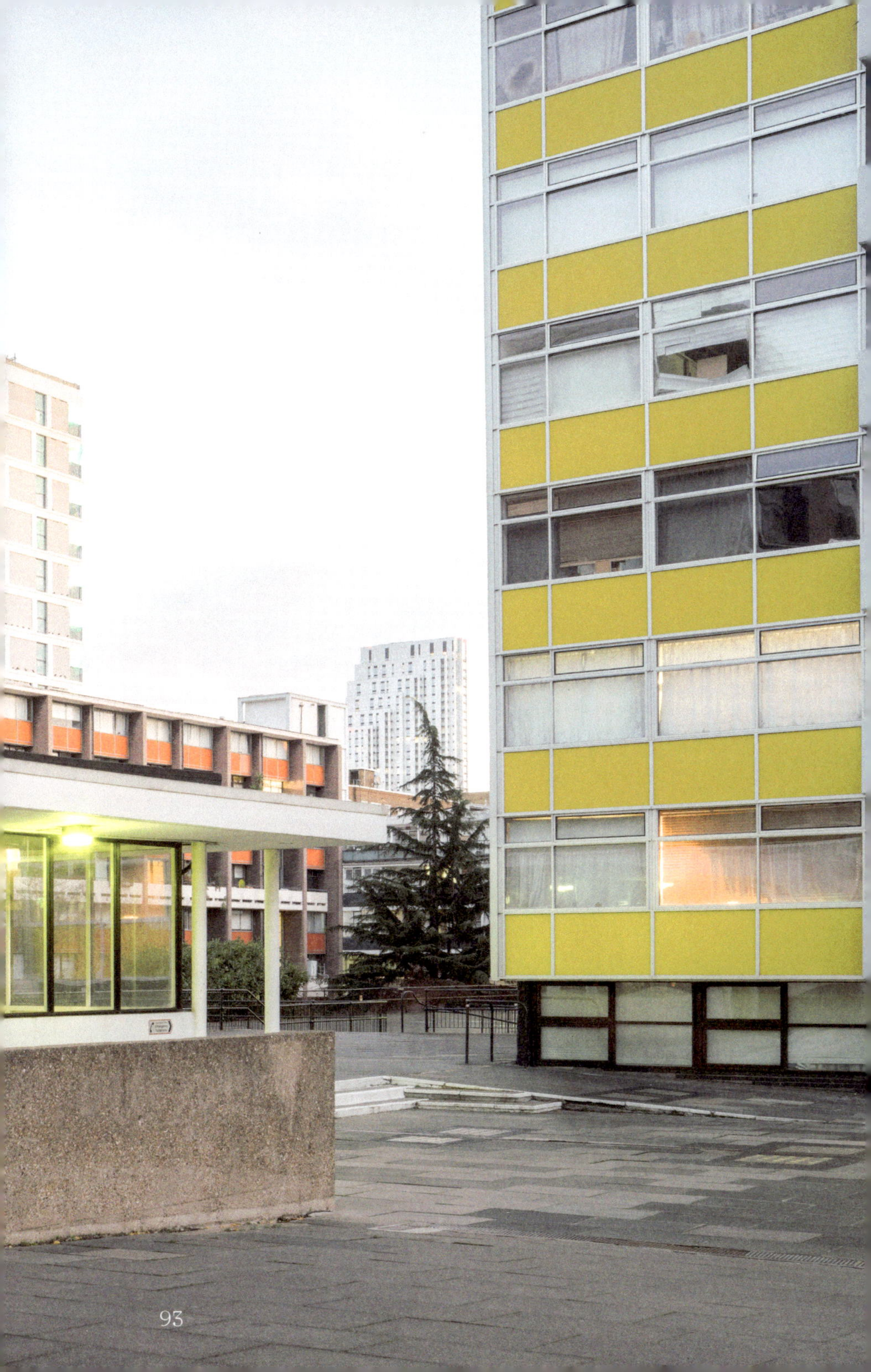

Previous Diaries

Cairo Diary #1
2014
ISBN 978-1-908889-20-1

Athens Diary #2
2015
ISBN 978-1-908889-29-4

Wolfsburg Diary #3
2016
ISBN 978-1-908889-34-8

Taipei Diary #4
2015
ISBN 978-1-908889-30-0

Kochi Diary #5
2018
ISBN 978-1-908889-44-7

Beirut Diary #6
2018
ISBN 978-1-908889-40-9

Wuhan Diary #7
2018
ISBN 978-1-908889-645

Zurich Diary #8
2019
ISBN 978-1-908889-65-2

Budapest Diary #9
2020
ISBN 978-1-908889-66-9

Osaka Diary #10
2020
ISBN 978-1-908889-56-0

Dhaka Diary #11
2021
ISBN 978-1-908889-86-7

Yangon Diary #12
2021
ISBN 978-1-908889-87-4

Minsk Diary #13
2021
ISBN 978-1-908889-88-1

Belfast Diary #14
2021
ISBN 978-1-908889-89-8

Linz Diary #15
2021
ISBN 978-1-908889-90-4

The previous diaries have been published by *thevelvetcell.com* and are available through the website.

George Town Diary #16
2022
ISBN 978-3-96070-090-6

Unna Diary #17
2022
ISBN 978-3-96070-089-0

Sarajevo Diary #18
2022
ISBN 978-3-96070-088-3

Bangkok Diary #19
2022
ISBN 978-3-96070-087-6

Kuching Diary #20
2024
ISBN 978-3-96070-105-7

Turin Diary #21
2024
ISBN 978-3-96070-103-3

Wilson Diary #22
2024
ISBN 978-3-96070-106-4

London Diary #23
2024
ISBN 978-3-96070-104-0

London Diary
Peter Bialobrzeski

Published by
Hartmann Books
Liststraße 28/1
70180 Stuttgart
hartmann-books.com

Photographs
Peter Bialobrzeski
bialobrzeski.net

Graphic Design and Typesetting
Sarah Fricke, Distaff Studio

Copyediting
Tas Skorupa, New York

Printing and Binding
DZA Druckerei zu Altenburg

Paper
Pergraphica Natural Rough

Typefaces
ABC Diatype, GT Alpina

First Edition, 2024
500 copies

ISBN
978-3-96070-104-0

For Raoul